Images or idols?

The place of sacred art in churches today

KEITH WALKER MA, BSc, PhD, FRSA

Canon Librarian of Winchester Cathedral

D1439583

The Canterbury ...
Norwich

J144/06

© A. Keith Walker 1996

First published 1996 by The Canterbury Press Norwich
(a publishing imprint of Hymns Ancient & Modern Limited,
a registered charity)
St Mary's Works, St Mary's Plain,
Norwich, Norfolk, NR3 3BH

British Library Cataloguing in Publication Data

A catalogue record for this book is available
from the British Library

ISBN 1–85311–134–1

*Typeset by David Gregson Associates, Beccles, Suffolk
Printed and bound in Great Britain by
Biddles Ltd, Guildford and King's Lynn*

BY THE SAME AUTHOR:

William Law, his Life and Work (1974, SPCK)

'And now that time grows shorter, I perceive
That Plato's is the truest poetry,
And that these shadows
Are cast by the true.'

Edwin Muir

CONTENTS

PREFACE

THE PURPOSE of this study is essentially practical. The general tone of the relationship between the Church and the visual arts, at least in England, but I suspect in most parts of the world, is one of estrangement. The same cannot be said of the relationship between the Church and music and if we consider the pre-Reformation Church and the arts as a whole the relationship mattered tremendously to most who were involved. What has happened in our cultural history to make the difference? Does it matter?

I believe that it does matter and that the Church and the visual arts all suffer because of the ignorance and hostility that fuel the estrangement. From the standpoint of the Church I believe that its mission is flawed unless it is able to embrace the ministry of the sacred visual artist. Unrelated to the Church I believe that the arts lack a credible principle of coherence and tend to fail in rising to the challenge of expressing the sacred.

The argument of this book, I hope, will engage the interest of artists and churchpeople alike. It is intended to be a serious contribution to a debate that needs to be more keen, but the language used is intentionally direct. Clergy and parochial church councils, members of diocesan advisory councils and fabric advisory committees, and their equivalents in non-Anglican churches, need to consider the rightful place of the sacred visual artist within the Church much more searchingly than is usually the case at the moment. Art historians, art critics and teachers need often to be more informed and fair about the significance of the Church, both historically and in its contemporary manifestation. All who care for the visual arts, for God, or for both, should care for the subject of this book. It will not always breed agreement but I trust it will stimulate thought and deepen perception.

I wish to thank Dr Julia Viersen for so cheerfully undertaking the laborious task of making a fair typescript from my dense pages.

INTRODUCTION

ON CHRISTMAS EVE, 1992, a 137 cm (4 ft 6 in) high plaster statue of the Blessed Virgin Mary holding the Child Jesus was introduced into the Anglican church of St Mary's, Cottingham, near Hull. It had been acquired by the Rector on a sale-or-return basis as a memorial to a recently deceased worshipper who had left £3,000 to the church. The statue came from a mould, brightly coloured and Italianate in style. It was made in about 1876 and its type is often found in Roman Catholic churches. Mary's eyes are cast down in simpering humility and her right hand points to the Child, whose arms are outstretched. In Mary the curse on our First Parents is reversed and the defeated serpent duly lies beneath her feet. So do clouds, for the Book of Revelation (chapter 12) speaks curiously of a woman and child which the Church identified with the Virgin and the Child Jesus.

Not all members of the church were happy with the new arrival. So much friction resulted in fact that a hearing took place in the consistory court before the Chancellor of the diocese. Thirty-five members of the congregation lodged formal objection to the retention of the statue. The petitioners, consisting of the Rector, churchwardens and Parochial Church Council (PCC) secretary insisted that the statue could only stand on a plinth as tall as itself, spotlighted and near the nave altar. The Chancellor advised that at the start of the project the petitioners should have consulted the church architect, the Diocesan Advisory Committee (DAC) and the congregation as a whole. The DAC secretary claimed that his Committee would have advised commissioning a new work rather than acceding to the stock item in question. Congregational objectors insisted that the Rector was trying to shift the belief and practice of the church too rapidly in a Catholic direction, and that the shift was illustrated in the present statue. The petitioners were ordered to pay costs of some thousands of pounds, but this money was vouchsafed by the numerous well-wishers in the congregation.[1]

This cautionary tale exemplifies many of the problems associated with trying to introduce visual art into the Church today. Although my attention is restricted mainly to the Church of England tales similar in substance could be told from other churches and from other countries. The Rector and his friends had the laudable desire to embellish their church with visual art and to do so with due regard for liturgical needs. The focus of Redemption was to be illustrated near the place of redeeming life. That controversy broke out is tribute to the power of visual images and the swift recognition of doctrinal truth or falsehood locked up in plaster and paint. Nor was the controversy simply religious. Aesthetic questions were raised but hardly answered by the Rector who defended his position by reference to an advisor who was not only ordained but had a degree in fine art. This fact seems only to compound the difficulty of appropriate embellishment.[2]

The pages that follow could be understood as a response to the issues raised by the Cottingham case. They arise in fact from a joyful and abrasive experience commissioning and being involved in commissioning new works of visual art in the service of the Church of England. It has been my privilege to have been intimately involved with Cecil Collins, Patrick Reyntiens, Edith Reyntiens, Elisabeth Collins, Elisabeth Frink, Peter Eugene Ball, Antony Gormley, Michael Renton, Sergei Fedorov and Simon Verity in the production of sacred visual art for the Church. I was much involved in securing a fine *Agnus Dei* by Eric Gill for a cathedral when it might easily have gone to a private collector or overseas. It has been another privilege to have worked with Dean Walter Hussey as his colleague during his final years at Chichester Cathedral.

The joy has been experienced because I recognised the task as high and urgent and the problems associated

---

1. *Church Times*, 18 March 1994
2. *Church Times*, 29 April 1994

with fund-raising, committee work, choice and encouragement of artist were simply the cost entailed in seeing new
creation come to birth, some figuration of Being that
preached good news, and knowing that the Church was
strengthening itself and embracing humanity and the
universe in such realisation.

The abrasion has been caused by the nature of the difficulty, rather than the difficulty itself, in winning sacred visual
art for the Church. I will argue in the pages to come that the
visual artist working for the Church is a minister of the
Church. He is prophet, pastor and teacher; but why is his
mission so often misunderstood and decried? How could it
be that when Epstein created his great sculpture *Consum-
matum Est* (1937) he wrote, 'I even imagine the setting for
the finished figure, a dim crypt, with a subdued light on the
semi-translucent alabaster', but could have little hope of it
ever being placed in a cathedral or basilica? Why was he
unable even to donate his totemic *Behold the Man* to Selby
Abbey where the Rector wanted it but others objected?[1] How
can it be in our own day that when Albert Herbert, a Roman
Catholic and one of our best painters, produced a series of
designs for the Stations of the Cross for an Anglican church
in London the commission was turned down because of the
unpleasantness of what was portrayed? The answer, in part
at least, will unfold in the pages to come.

Attention has been focussed on the Church of England for
three reasons. First, I know it best and what happens in other
churches is unlikely significantly to differ. Second, almost all
the pre-Reformation churches belong to the Church of
England and they are the greatest sacred visual art the nation
possesses. Third, whilst it would be politically correct to
include non-Christian religious art in this country, by and
large that art has not yet established itself nationally as
significant, nor are the adherents of non-Christian religions
generally numerous. The newly opened Hindu mandir in

1. E. Silber, *Jacob Epstein*, Sculpture and Drawings Leeds City and Whitechapel Art
Galleries 1987. See also *Epstein, An Autobiography*, 1955, which contains many
illustrations of ecclesiastical and secular misunderstanding of his sacred art.

Neasden, London is impressive but unlike almost every other
sacred building in the land.

According to the HMSO *Social Trends (24)* there are 58
million people in Great Britain. 500,000 are Muslims, 250,000
are Sikhs, 140,000 are Hindus, 110,000 are Jews, and there
are 80,000 members of other non-Christian religions. This
amounts to 1.9% of the population. 65% of the population
adopts some form of trinitarian religion; 46% say that they
are Anglican, 10% say that they are Roman Catholic and
500,000 adopt a non-trinitarian form of the Christian religion.

There are 16,502 churches in England, 12,772 are listed,
2,902 are Grade 1 listed (comprising 47.5% of all Grade 1
buildings), and there are 8,500 pre-Reformation churches,
including the great cathedrals. It follows from this that
churches are among our most precious artefacts and an
Anglican predominance is part of the evidence.

Despite the centuries' long decay in the tradition of visual
art in sacred places, and the difficulties encountered in
commissioning significant new work, this is an optimistic
book. The best new work is excellent. Theologians in recent
decades have given new attention to the subject. I think of
such writers as Von Balthasar, Paul Tillich, John Dillenberger,
Jane Dillenberger, Edward Robinson, Horton Davies, H. R.
Rookmaker, Jeremy Begbie, George Pattison and the interesting religious atheist who had not finished his spiritual
journey before his premature death, Peter Fuller. Most of all
I will argue that we are in an age of transition and the
predominant materialistic base of our culture is in process of
changing to a metaphysical base. Involved in that change,
both as agent and consequence sacred art will increase in
vitality and productiveness. In the metaphysical age to come
it will be one of the glories of the time.

1. What the Tradition Teaches Us

THREE SOURCES informed the first Christians' understanding of sacred visual art. The Graeco-Roman culture of which they were a part gave the form, the Old Testament gave some of the content, and their experience of Christ within the Church, coupled with writings that became eventually the New Testament completed their understanding. We shall begin with the Bible as a whole in considering the tradition, for whilst this is not chronologically quite accurate it is convenient and the first Christians had increasing access to authoritative writings which became eventually the Bible.

THE BIBLE

It seems likely that visual art and sacred visual art had significance for the Jews until the prophetic condemnations of Hosea led to the banning of sacred images in the Deuteronomic reforms of the seventh century BC. Whilst scholars are not unanimously in agreement it seems likely that images were to be found on the Ark, the ephod[1], the teraphim[2] and the pole, whilst the brazen serpent was clearly an image[3]. The little golden bulls set up at Bethel as representations of Yahweh would seem to have lasted until the time of Hosea[4]. The epiphany of God from out of the burning bush[5] and the encounter of Moses from the crevice of a rock where he was permitted to see the back of God, but not his face, are not sacred art, but they are God made accessible through nature, imagination, nature mysticism and analogy, which are very close to visual art.

The Second Commandment, however, had a decisive effect on Old Testament humanity, and subsequently on the

1. Judges 8.26–27
2. Judges 18.14, 17–19
3. Numbers 21.8–9
4. Kings 12.28
5. Exodus 3.3, 4

tradition of the Church. It reads, 'You must not make a carved image for yourself, nor the likeness of anything in the heavens above, nor on the earth below, or in the waters under the earth. You must not bow down to them in worship; for "I, the Lord your God, am a jealous God ..."'[1] The original reference is to sculptured forms, but it came to include any cultic image. Isaiah summed up the prophetic understanding, which became orthodox, when he cried, 'You will treat as things unclean your silver-plated images and your gold-covered idols; you will loathe them like a foul discharge and call them filth'.[2] According to M. McKeating, 'By the Graeco-Roman period the prohibition was held to rule out any artistic representation of animal or human figures in any medium whatever'.[3]

It must seem strange that Israel should come to adopt a rule so much at variance with the practice of surrounding nations and basic human drives. It is interesting that the verb in Hebrew for 'to paint' does not exist, and some have suggested that Hebrews are congenitally deficient in visual sensitivity. This seems to me extremely unlikely partly because of the wonderful art of such Jews as Lipchitz, Epstein and Chagall, partly because of the brilliant artistic imagination illustrated in the verbal images of the Bible and its narrative theology, and partly because there is evidence of visual sacred art prior to the enforcement of a religious and civil rule.

It may be that the long years of nomadic existence gave insufficient support for the development of visual art as a cultural activity, but the decisive factor must have been the mentality that gave rise to the Second Commandment. Two powerful religious factors were at work. First, little, disregarded Israel had a lofty vision of the reality of God. Israel understood, after rudimentary beginnings, that God is beyond human conceiving, that he is other than the energies of nature. His presence may be known in nature and history

1. Exodus 20.4, 5 (REB)
2. 30.22 (REB)
3. *A New Dictionary of Christian Theology*, p. 280, SCM Press 1983

but in his essence he is transcendent. For this reason the Holy of Holies was empty; no image could represent God. With the passage of time Jews became reluctant even to name him, so unique and other was God felt to be. Second, Israel believed itself to be the Chosen People and their God was the true God, eventually the only God. The holy images of surrounding nations were seen in consequence as distractions, temptations and sources of pollution. Wayward Jews turned to such idols and their religion became compromised. The prophetic movement reinforced the separateness of Israel and castigated syncretism as the prostitution of true religion, meriting the wrath of God.

This aniconic religious view is carried over into the New Testament. There is a dread of being infected by idolatrous forms of worship[1]. More typically, however, the idea of idolatry is spiritualised as we are counselled, for example, not to make an idol of gain[2].

Scholarly discussions of the biblical view of sacred visual art rarely go further than this, but it seems to me that we can go much further. What are we to make of the extraordinary perception of Jesus, 'Consider how the lilies grow in the fields; they do not work, they do not spin; yet I tell you, even Solomon in all his splendour was not attired like one of them'[3]? Carlyle, who quotes these words in his essay on the *Hero as Poet*, says of their author, 'A glance, that, into the deepest deep of Beauty'.[4] Whilst it has been said with some justice that St Paul journeyed through some of the world's finest scenery nothing to its glory is mentioned in his letters, he in fact echoes Jesus in saying, 'Ever since the world began his [God's] invisible attributes, that is to say his everlasting power and deity, have been visible to the eye of reason, in the things he has made'.[5] Not only are such remarks far from moralism and narrow salvationism, they are in the realm of

1. 1 Corinthians 8.8–13; Revelation 2.14, 20
2. Ephesians 5.5
3. Matthew 6.28, 29
4. *Lectures on Heroes*, Lecture 3, p. 245, London
5. Romans 1.20 (REB); Dodd translates 'quite perceptible' for 'visible to the eye of reason'

aesthetics and regard for beauty. Further, there is the clear
recognition of the invisible coming to light through the
visible in the natural world. The artist may well see what
Jesus and Paul saw and his art may well be a means of
helping the rest of us to see with clearer eyes. Jane
Dillenberger quotes the thought and experience of Bernard
Berenson, the famous art critic and connoisseur, as follows,
'In visual art the aesthetic moment is that flitting instant, so
brief as to be almost timeless, when the spectator is at one
with the work he is looking at ... When he recovers
workaday consciousness it is as if he had been initiated into
illuminating, exalting, formative mysteries. In short, the
aesthetic moment is a moment of mystic vision'.[1] Professor
Dillenberger then quotes an experience of Berenson when
he had been gazing for hours at Chinese landscapes in
Detroit and, getting up to leave the museum found himself
looking through a window at trees. He cried out, 'Look,
look, these trees are the finest yet!' Art had elevated his
consciousness to see something about which Jesus and Paul
spoke.

Then there is the kind of personality we find in Jeremiah
and the other prophets, in Jesus and Paul. Their vocabulary
is richly poetic and dramatic action is a means of communi-
cating truth. The level of inspiration in the prophets and Paul
may be higher and directed to a more crucial purpose than
those of most artists but they all seem to draw from the same
dimension of reality. The reader must read the lives and
words of those mentioned to discover this. It is enough to
recall Jeremiah wearing a yoke to symbolise the approaching
servitude of the heedless Jews and the poetic form of his
utterance[2], the teaching of Jesus in parables, and Paul's hymn
to love[3] in relation to which scholars say that it was probably
a spontaneous utterance and that as he spoke Paul must
have had before the eye of his heart the image of the
Crucified.

---

1. *Style and Content in Christian Art*, pp. 25–6, SCM Press 1986
2. Jeremiah 28; 30; 31, etc
3. 1 Corinthians 13

There are important extensions of this point. The whole movement of the life of Jesus is in some sense holy theatre. What he says and what he does are of one piece and a communication to others. This is especially true of the Passion, Crucifixion and Resurrection. The institution of the eucharist at the Last Supper indicates plainly that Jesus believed that the truth could be acted and that grace could be transmitted through visible things and action. E. J. Tinsley in a book that has not received the attention it deserves, *The Imitation of God in Christ*[1], argues that Jesus saw his life as an enactment of the Way of Israel. This way is summed up and consummated in him and meditation on this model way opens the possibility for the rest of us to enter into the way of truth. St Paul understood this point when he declared to the wayward Corinthians, 'Follow my example as I follow Christ's'.[2] The Greek word at the root of this thought is that from which we derive the English verb 'to mime'. Not only is miming an important expression of dramatic art, it is what acting consists in, and is deeply involved in the creation of visual art. It has been said that Picasso re-worked the history of western painting. The parallel with the New Testament conception is exact, because repetition and historical imitation would be a mistake in either case. The disciple meditates on the life of Christ to discover the way of humanity and thus his own way. The love and humility into which he is called simply releases his own humanity to be authentically creative. Similarly the actor and painter become themselves through that which engages their attention and it comes to life through them.

If this point is true we can say that what we see in Jesus is a reflection of the way of God. The Bible is narrative theology illustrating how we enter into truth through attention to history and experience of it. Thus God is the original artist and human artists reflect in their way his way. An

---

1. SCM Press 1960
2. 1 Corinthians 11.1. For the frequency of the appeal see 1 Thessalonians 1.6; 2.14; 2 Thessalonians 3.7; 3.9; 1 Corinthians 4.16; Phillippians 3.17; Ephesians 5.1; also Hebrews 6.12; 13.7; 3 John v.11

archetypal reality runs through all things as Plato and the author of the Fourth Gospel recognised. It is this reality of which a classicist like E. V. Rieu was aware when he began to translate the gospels for the Penguin series of classics and discovered that his wrestling with the text brought him into relation with the subject and eventually conversion. He records, 'Of what I have learnt from these documents in the course of my long task, I will say nothing now. Only this, that they bear the seal of the Son of Man and God, they are the Magna Carta of the human spirit. Were we to devote to their comprehension a little of the selfless enthusiasm that is now expended on the riddle of our physical surroundings, we should cease to say that Christianity is coming to an end – we might even feel that it had only just begun.'[1]

We are led naturally to the Incarnation. The Latin root of the word means 'enfleshing'. With the interest of this book in mind we might say that it is consonant with the metaphor of God as the author of the drama of creation, as the artist painting the canvas of existing things, that he should give himself to that which he is creating. The Christian belief is that in the person of Jesus he has done that. We may say that an incarnating principle is at work in all art and in the unfolding of all religion and the Jewish and Christian religions in particular. The difference in Christianity is the scandal of particularity, the belief that echoes become actual voice, shadows real presence. The Incarnation receives an illumination from art in another way. No artist paints 'Beauty', the general principle. He paints a flower or a young girl and as we look at this particular the general reality of beauty is apparent to us. It is appropriate to our way of human learning that as we meditate on this particular, Christ, we are drawn into the reality of God.

We are left with the response made to Jesus by those who met him and the response we make to the Bible and to the enrichment of the Bible we call the Church. Once more what is asked of us is strangely akin to what is asked by the artist in relation to his work. The sculptor Edward Robinson

---

1. E. V. Rieu, Introduction *The Four Gospels*, pp. xxxii–xxxiii, Penguin, 1952

quoting a fellow artist writes, 'he calls for "what happens in creative labour to be repeated in the listener's perception". If, that is, instead of remaining passively receptive we shall find powers both of discovery and invention being brought to the surface in ourselves, like those seeds long buried too deep to germinate. Only then does the real work of art, the work that is art, conceived of as a never-ending interaction between creative artist and creative listener, reader, viewer – only then does that work of art really come to life; only then does it continue to have a life of its own; to survive, because of the work we have done to fertilise it. In Naum Gabo's words, "it only attains full stature with what people and time make of it". So King Lear was not left by Shakespeare as a finished work of art; it has continually to be re-created, its infinite possibilities continually brought to light by those who bring their own experience of life to its interpretation. As they perform it, so must I perform, I must re-create myself, a Brancusi bronze, a poem by Seamus Heaney. What I may then call the beauty of such a work is a measure of the creative energy it can generate and release in myself.'[1] Thus Jesus is asked a question and he replies with a parable and the listener is asked to interpret and respond to what he has heard[2]. Such is the fecundity of the Bible that in every generation artists and scholars interpret and re-interpret what can be read. Christian belief demands meditation and commitment, commitment and meditation. It seems that God has ordered things much the same, whether in art or religious knowledge.

THE EARLY TRADITION OF THE CHURCH

The first Christians met in the synagogue with fellow Jews and together in one another's homes. Soon they split from the Jews because of the unwillingness of the main body of Jews to accept Christian claims. As an illicit religion within the Roman Empire Christians met secretly, and modesty was

1. *Icons of the Present*, p. 64, SCM Press 1993
2. For example Luke 10.25–37

enjoined upon them. Little has come down to us from pre-
Constantinian days due to the hazards of time and the somewhat furtive life Christians were forced to live. The writings
of the early Church Fathers are more plentiful and Sister
Mary Charles Murray[1] and other scholars have helped us to
understand that the older theory, whereby it was understood
that the leaders of the Church out of respect for the Second
Commandment of the Decalogue and pure, spiritual religion
banned sacred image, is untrue. It seems that the Second
Commandment was either ignored or spiritualised to mean
that we must avoid idolatry of the heart or the worship,
rather than reverence, of images. Tertullian can condemn
them, but his position is normally extreme and in other
places he accepts them. Examining the literary evidence
from Tertullian to Paulinus of Nola Sister Charles Murray
concludes, 'it seems a reasonable assessment of the case to
say that there is very little indication indeed that the Fathers
of the early Church were in any way opposed to art'.[2]

The evidence of artefacts suggests that it was normal for
Christians to decorate places reserved for worship. The
house church found at the frontier town of Dura-Europos
has various biblical scenes; the Samaritan woman with Jesus
at the well, David and Goliath, and the woman at the empty
tomb. The sarcophagus of Junius Bassus depicts in sculptured form Abraham and Isaac, Paul being arrested, Christ
seated between Peter and Paul giving them responsibility for
the church, Jesus arraigned before Pilate, Pilate preparing to
wash his hands, Job seated on the ash heap, Adam and Eve
at the time of the fall, Jesus' entry into Jerusalem, Daniel in
the lion's den, Paul led away to execution. There are 550
miles of catacombs beneath Rome and Christians sheltering
there and burying their dead with appropriate rituals
decorated the walls. Although there are no certain artistic
remains from before the mid-second century we find in the
catacomb of Priscilla from the third century a painting of
Mary and Jesus. In the catacomb of Callistus we find the

---

1. *Journal of Theological Studies*, vol. xxviii, pt 2, October 1977
2. Op. cit. p. 342

Baptism of Jesus and the woman at the well. The fourth century catacomb of Sts Peter and Marcellino give us Christ, the Good Shepherd, other biblical images and decoration. They follow the form of Graeco-Roman art. None of them are remarkable aesthetically, but they prove the importance of the visual as a parallel language to the verbal from the earliest period and that the visual was integrated with liturgy and prayer.[1]

THE EASTERN TRADITION

Christianity became a licit religion within the Roman Empire and received the official support of the Emperor Constantine in AD 312. In about AD 330 he moved the capital of the Empire from Rome to Byzantium, soon to be re-named Constantinople. Legality and the favour of the Emperor led to an explosion of church building and decoration, all the more so when Christianity became the sole legitimate religion. The culture out of which this art grew was now eastern rather than Graeco-Roman and in this fact lies an essential difference between western Catholic and Orthodox art. Activisim and order typical of the Aristotelian west is replaced in the east by contemplation and a Platonist view of the universe. The form of church architecture typical of the east is apparent already in the Hagia Sophia, built in the sixth century in Constantinople. By about the year AD 1,000 the pattern of Orthodox church buildings had been finally settled as a circle above a square which now became a Greek cross. The roof and walls are divided into a series of zones. The figure of Christ, usually a Pantocrator (Ruler of All) dominates the interior from the dome above, a figure of the Blessed Virgin Mary adorns the apse. In the upper zones are scenes from the life of Christ and especially the Passion, below, the portraits of saints. The life of the Blessed Virgin Mary and local saints are located in side chapels. Mosaics,

1. Illustrations and commentary can be found in A. Toynbee (ed), *The Crucible of Christianity*, pp. 172–193; 216–224, Thames and Hudson, 1969; Jane Dillenberger, *Style and Content in Christian Art*, plates and p. 29; John Dillenberger, *A Theology of Artistic Sensibilities*, pp. 3–20

frescos and icons are the typical form of church decoration. It is significant of the joy and beauty of the Christian revelation that wall mosaics, using glass tesserae, seem to have been a Christian invention. Mosaics were known to the Sumerians in c. 3,000 BC and were used by Hellenistic Greeks and Romans, but they used small cubes of marble in plaster. Normally they were laid as a floor and did not shine. H. W. Janson writes, 'The vast and intricate wall mosaics of Early Christian art thus was essentially without precedent. The same is true of their material, for they consist of tesserae made of coloured glass ... All these qualities made glass mosaic the ideal complement of the new architectural aesthetic that confronts us in Early Christian basilicas.'[1]

• Research into the origin of the icon still proceeds. Attention has been called to the remarkable Fayum portraits which originated at the Fayum oasis in the Egyptian desert. These paintings are creations of simple and extraordinary beauty. Positioned frontally the head and shoulders are depicted in idealised form with faces that seem to gaze into eternity. They date from the first to the fourth centuries of our era. The painters would seem to have belonged to a gnostic or mystical sect common in the area.[2]

Icon painting is a canonical art that has changed little in the course of centuries. The tradition was passed down from master to pupil and different regions and times show variations on the fundamental theme. Between 1730 and 1734 Dionysius of Fourna compiled from various sources and published his *Painter's Manual*[3] which gives us an insight into the icon painter's understanding. Prayer and the service of the Church are emphasised as preparatory qualities. A particular icon must be painted according to certain rules and this relates not only to materials and the preparation of the surface but to iconography. This is what he writes for painting the *Nativity of Christ*: 'a cave, with inside it on the

---

1. H. W. Janson, *History of Art*, p. 260, 4th ed. 1991
2. R. Temple, *Icons and the Mystical Origins of Christianity*, ch. 8, Element Books, 1990
3. Translated by P. Hetherington, Sagittarius Press, 1974

right the Mother of God kneeling and laying the infant Christ, wrapped in swaddling clothes, in the crib; on the left Joseph is kneeling with his hands crossed on his breast. Behind the crib an ox and an ass are looking at Christ and behind Joseph and the Virgin are shepherds holding staves and also looking with wonder at Christ. Outside the cave are sheep and shepherds, one of them playing on a flute and others looking up with fear, while above them an angel blesses them. On the other side the Magi on horseback in royal clothes are showing each other the star. Above the cave a crowd of angels in the clouds hold a scroll with these words, "Glory to God in the highest, and on earth peace, goodwill towards men". And in the midst of them is the star, with a broad ray coming down onto the head of Christ.'[1] Hetherington traces the sources of the scene to pseudo-Matthew, pseudo-Luke and the Gospels. The flute-player may be an invention of Hellenistic artists interpreting a phrase in the Greek Night Office for Christmas Eve. The omission of reference to mid-wives may reflect a wish to limit accumulated tradition.

The earliest known icon of Christ dates from the sixth century. The paucity of early icons is due mainly to the destruction occasioned during the Iconoclastic Controversy which ravaged Christendom and especially Eastern Christendom from AD 726–835. The roots of this controversy, the type of which occurs from time to time in Christian history, are as follows: a strong transcendentalist belief despised attempts to represent the invisible deity and heavenly creatures; a strong ascetisim minimised outward, physical representations; a moralism felt money spent on such icons might have been better diverted to the relief of the poor; Arianism in its different forms thought that Christ, the Virgin and allied subjects should not be honoured in so divine or sanctified a manner; in the tension between Church and state the Emperor and his party resented the split allegiance represented by the honour paid to endless icons of Christ, King of Kings.

1. Op. cit. p. 32

St John Damascene, writing in Palestine, and therefore protected from Christian wrath by Muslim rule, wrote *Defense of Holy Images* which answered definitively objections to icons and has remained authoritative in Orthodox thinking since the eighth century when it was written. He argues that as the Church is infallible the tradition of icon painting must be correct; that whilst the invisible God is not represented in the Old Testament a change has come with the Incarnation. 'I do not draw an icon of the invisible Godhead, but I paint an icon of the flesh of God which was seen'; the Old Testament image prohibition was due to the danger of idolatry. If images are not worshipped there can be no offence; an icon is a likeness with a difference. 'An icon is a likeness which exhibits the characteristics of a prototype from which it differs in some particular respect.' (It was well known that St Basil had written, 'The honour paid to the image passes to the prototype'); there are different types of veneration, the veneration of worship, due to God alone, the veneration of God's friends and the veneration of humans according to appropriate honour (the Orthodox more generally distinguish worship due to God alone from veneration. The word venerate comes from the Greek words meaning 'to embrace and kiss' and 'lovingly'); icons sanctify the sense of sight by God's energy. 'What the discourse is to hearing, that the icon is to sight'; Christ, the Virgin and the saints are depicted because God glorifies those who glorify him. The energy of the Holy Spirit remains in icons as in the souls and bodies of the sanctified and divine. At a later date Theodore of Studios made two interesting remarks. He wrote, 'Man himself is created after the image and likeness of God, therefore there is something divine in the art of making images'. He also believed it to be necessary, 'As perfect man Christ not only can but must be represented and worshipped in images: let this be denied and Christ's economy of salvation is virtually destroyed'. The Council of Nicaea, AD 787 safeguarded orthodoxy by ruling, 'the composition of religious pictures is not left to the inspiration of artists, but depends on the principles laid down by the Catholic Church and religious tradition. Art alone is the painter's province, the composition belongs to the Fathers.' [1]

Icons take many forms. The early ones had a sliding lid to protect them during travel. The diptych, invented as a writing tablet, was used to display two icons and this led naturally to the triptych. Although wood is the usual base for the paint it is not mandatory. In some periods gold and silver or precious stones have been used to enhance the painted surface. Cloisonné enamel has been especially favoured. A flat surface is preferred, however, because it reduces the idea of corporeality. For this reason statuary has never thrived in Orthodox churches.

The iconostasis is of particular importance. It can convey an enormous sense of spiritual beauty. The iconostasis divides the sanctuary from the main body of the church. It is a natural focal point for icons. A deesis (supplication) forms the necessary minimum representation. It consists of Christ the Teacher in the middle, Mary the Mother of God and John the Baptist on either side, with local saints possibly added. This scheme may be augmented by scenes from the life of Christ, angels, feasts and doctors and saints of the Church. By the thirteenth century the Royal Doors at the centre, through which the sanctuary party process towards the congregation with the eucharistic elements, were decorated with the Annunciation. Theophanes the Greek, Dionysius and Andrei Rublev are sometimes regarded as the greatest icon painters. In the case of Rublev icon painting attained an unsurpassed lyrical serenity and grace, where dematerialised bodies are defined in flowing, rhythmic lines and gentle, harmonious colours. It is important to note that Rublev has been canonised by the Orthodox Church. In the west Fra Angelico was beatified in 1984, but in general visual artists have been little honoured by the Church.

The westernising enthusiasm of Peter the Great in the seventeenth century led to the adulterating of the essential spirit of icon painting by Western artistic principles. Communism devastated the heritage but the genuine art is being

1. J. Gimpel, *The Cathedral Builders*, Pimlico, p. 84, 1993

revived in Russia and a new love of icons is to be found throughout the west. They appear in churches and cathedrals of Roman and Anglican conviction in Europe and in the United States of America. Numerous scholarly and popular studies are written and cheap reproductions of icons can be bought readily. The Victoria and Albert Museum 'Gates of Mystery' exhibition of Russian Icons in 1993 took everybody by surprise as over 67,000 people visited it in three months. One major reviewer contrasted the distorted features to be found in the paintings of Francis Bacon, on show in another gallery, with the noble and uplifting images of the icons, and John McEwen began his laudatory review by relating a number of instances of violence that had occurred within his personal experience during the previous few days and contrasted the disjointed nature of our culture with the inspired world of the icon.

In the life of St Stephen the Younger (d.765) we read, 'The icon is a door'. Those who treasure icons believe that by contemplating them they are brought into the presence of the subject depicted on the icon. They believe also that the prayer through which the icon is partly made gives to the icon a living quality so that the transformation of matter, to be accomplished at the Last Day, has already begun. The implications for our understanding of the environment to be drawn from this perception are enormous.

THE WESTERN CHURCH

The form of church buildings in the west after the Peace of Constantine in the fourth century was suggested by the secular basilica used for the exercise of justice. The pagan temples were thought to be polluted by evil spirits and were avoided. St John Lateran, Santa Maria Maggiore and other great churches in Rome give us apt examples. The essential style markedly strong in the Church of the Nativity in Bethlehem has architecturally pronounced horizontal lines. The high altar is at the east end and columns divide the nave north and south. Pope Leo the Great in the fifth century saw the value of ecclesiastical painting as a means of instruction for the illiterate populace and cycles of paintings illustrating the life of Jesus, Paul and the great doctrines of the faith with appropriate decorative additions appeared increasingly on the walls and vaults of churches. Pope Gregory the Great in the sixth century, soon to be made a Doctor of the Church, said, 'The image is to the illiterate what scripture is to those who can read, for in the image even the illiterate can see what they have to ... there those who never learned are able to read.'[1] This view became determinative for Western Catholicism. Since the point is critical for our final evaluation of sacred visual art we may add three later testimonies. In the early twelfth century Theophilus, alias Roger of Helmarshausen, wrote, 'if a faithful soul should see the representation of the Lord's crucifixion expressed in the strokes of an artist, it is itself pierced, if it sees how great are the tortures that the saints have endured in their bodies and how great the rewards of eternal life that they have received, it grasps at the observance of a better life; if it contemplates how great are the joys in heaven and how great are the torments in the flames of hell, it is inspired with hope because of its good deeds and shaken with fear on considering its sins'.[2] In the fifteenth century John Myrc declared, 'I say boldly that there are many thousands of people that could not imagine in their hearts how Christ was crucified if they did not learn it by looking at sculpture and painting'.[3] Mantegna, the great Renaissance painter said, respecting sacred figures painted in churches, 'more than history itself or sermons, so strong and vehement a spur and good is there in painting that urges to the emulation of their worth'.[4]

Having sketched the principles animating the great eastern and western traditions at the outset of the Church's life it is not my intention to complete the sketch with a record of the intervening centuries. Instead I shall select episodes that illuminate the place of visual art in today's Church, with special reference to the Church of England. The Dark Ages began to

1. Epistle 2.13
2. *On Divers Arts*, p. 79, Dover Publications, 1979
3. Quoted S. Haskins, *Mary Magdalen*, pp. 193–4, Harper Collins, 1993
4. R. Lightbrown, *Mantegna*, p. 940, Phaidon, 1986

recede with the advent of Charlemagne, the Carolingian Revival and the Ottonian flowering which, with the brilliant Celtic art of Ireland and Britain supported the Church until the more familiar Romanesque period, beginning in the eleventh century. Charlemagne gave shelter and work to Byzantine artists who sought to gain his favour as a consequence of the Iconoclastic Dispute. Visitors to the Palatine Chapel at Aachen can see the splendid fruits of his endeavours in the magnificent, somewhat Byzantine style chapel and its rich but discrete ornamentation. This period saw the cutting of the Lothair Cross and the carving of the Gero Cross, two high points in the perfect blending of art and religious feeling.

In the eleventh century came the Romanesque period. Classical, Byzantine, Barbarian, Carolingian and Ottonian influences co-mingled at a time when 'the whole earth ... was clothing itself everywhere in the white robe of the Church'.[1] But the sacred visual art of the period had its ecclesiastical critics. St Bernard of Clairvaux looked with different eyes than ourselves upon the achievement of Moissac, Autun, Vezelay and Southwell. St Bernard (d.1153) was devout, austere and orthodox. In 1830 he was declared a Doctor of the Church and already Dante placed him near to the Blessed Virgin Mary in the hierarchy of the blessed. St Bernard was also eloquent and his conflict with Abbot Suger is instructive.

Abbot Suger was a man of enormous energy and enterprise. He was profoundly moved by the beauty of existent things. He became the most important instigator of the Gothic phase of architecture and this was possible because he supervised the Abbey Church of St Denis near Paris. The abbey needed repair but Suger took the opportunity to rebuild the apse and west end, modify the nave, add brilliant stained glass, employ sculptors on statuary, create a great jewelled cross, textiles and much more. In this 'destructively creative enterprise' (the phrase is that of Erwin Panovsky)[2],

1. Raoul Glaber, 1002–3
2. Esaay Abbot Suger of Saint-Denis in *Meaning in the Visual Arts*, p. 168, Penguin, 1970

Suger was inspired by the writings of Dionysius the Aeropagiate, mistakenly identifying this fifth century Syrian Christian neo-platonist with the disciple of St Paul, whom he thought to be the missionary of France and Patron of his abbey. Dionysius believed in the Great Chain of Being. God gave birth to the whole creation as little by little it spread out beneath him in darker and denser modules, the more creation descended towards the weakest elements. By a wonderful magnetism, however, that which is lower in the hierarchy of being can ascend the scale and return to God by absorbing the light in created things and being thus transformed. Predominantly material light becomes more immaterial as one ascends the scale of being. Panovsky quotes words of Suger that he believes must be a direct reminiscence: 'When – out of my delight in the beauty of the house of God – the loveliness of the many-coloured stones has called me away from external cares, and worthy meditation has induced me to reflect, transferring that which is material to that which is immaterial, on the diversity of the sacred virtues: then it seems to me that I see myself dwelling, as it were, in some strange region of the universe which neither exists entirely in the slime of the earth nor entirely in the purity of Heaven; and that, by the grace of God, I can be transported from this inferior to that higher world in an angogical [i.e. mystical] manner'.[1]

Suger's world-affirming mysticism was countered by St Bernard's world – denying mysticism. The man who could ride on the shores of Lake Geneva and be unconscious of the natural beauty surrounding him writes thus: 'In the cloisters, under the eyes of the brethren engaged in reading, what business has there that ridiculous monstrosity, that amazing misshapen shapeliness? Those unclean monkeys? Those fierce lions? Those monstrous centaurs? Those semi-human beings? Those spotted tigers? Those fighting warriors? Those huntsmen blowing their horns? Here you behold several bodies beneath one head; there again several heads upon one body. Here you see a quadruped with the tail of a serpent; there a

1. Op. cit., p. 162

fish with the head of a quadruped. In fine, on all side there appears as rich and amazing a variety of forms that it is more delightful to read the marbles than the manuscripts, and to spend the whole day in admiring these things, piece by piece, rather than in meditating on the Law Divine'.[1] Such men could clearly never agree and it is fortunate for us that by political arrangement Suger was left in peace by Bernard. Bernard perhaps was never at peace. It is clear from this extract of his writing that he was much affected by what he condemned. On other occasions he called attention to the needs of the poor in comparison with the wealth poured into unnecessarily large and sumptuous churches.

The thirteenth century saw the rise of Gothic, thought by some to be the most perfect expression of Christian art. Chartres Cathedral is the pre-eminent embodiment of the Gothic spirit and possibly Europe's greatest building. Otto von Simson has stressed 'the dual symbolism of the cathedral, which is at once a "model" of the cosmos and an image of the Celestial city'.[2] Geometry was the basis of the art of the builders, but they were well versed in the biblical writings about Solomon's Temple, and what is found in Ezekiel, Enoch and Revelation concerning the new or heavenly Temple. They took careful measurements of plants, stars and humans but their sacred geometry is still something of a mystery to us.

The present cathedral at Chartres is the fourth on the site and the building we observe was erected largely in thirty years. It is dedicated to the Blessed Virgin Mary, her cult having grown rapidly in medieval times, partly because she was a woman, and the worshipper longs to find the feminine associated with God, and partly because she was understood to be the refuge of sinners. The sculptured grouping representing the Last Judgement was found usually in the tympanum above the west doors of Romanesque churches and cathedrals. In medieval times we tend to find the Dormition, the Assumption and the Coronation of the

1. Quoted Panovsky, p. 166
2. *The Gothic Cathedral*, Introduction, Pantheon Books, 2nd Ed. 1962

Blessed Virgin Mary. She is very evident at Chartres, in stone and glass. Donations by pilgrims supplied much of the money for the building and this reminds us that the population at large was probably very much in favour of this enriched church. It held the tunic supposedly belonging to Mary and it became a popular goal of pilgrims.

According to Joseph Campbell 'The idea of a temple (or European Cathedral) is what is here announced, an enclosure wherein every feature is metaphorical of a connoted metaphysical intuition, set apart for ritual enactments'.[1] The same thought is expressed more compactly by Dionysius the Areopagite: 'the mason looks at the archetypes, grasps the divine model, and makes an impression of it in real material'. The different dimensions to the idea of seeing are certainly inescapable in the experience of a great medieval cathedral. In matters of moment the medievals distinguished four levels of seeing. There was the literal, let us say the cathedral building, and there was the mystical or allegorical. The mystical or allegorical was commonly divided into three parts. First and confusingly came the allegorical, in this case seeing the human heart reflected in the building and vice versa. Second, the moral, in this case the conversion of the disordered human heart into the divine order displayed by the cathedral. Lastly, there is the anagogical or mystical proper, in this case the recognition of the cathedral as a symbol of God's Kingdom and participation in its beatitude.

Some such depth to the idea of seeing is inescapable for a religious culture. It is entailed in a Platonic philosophy and typically in St John's gospel there is a constant play on the different meanings of the word 'seeing' most apparent in the story of the man born blind, made to see by Jesus, who then discovers that the religious authorities who can see the physical world and believe that they can see religious truth, are blind to that truth, expressed in and by Jesus[2]. Despite the difficulty of pretending to know what people 500 years ago might have experienced walking through a great cathedral

1. *Reflections on the Art of Living*, A. Joseph Campbell Companion, Selected and Edited by D. K. Osborn, p. 256, Harper Collins, 1991
2. Cf. Ch. 9

let us briefly attempt the exercise to illuminate our whole theme, and recognising that persons until the Enlightenment were very likely to have thought and felt in similar terms, at least in Catholic countries.

THE MEDIEVAL EXPERIENCE

The pilgrim would see in his journey to the cathedral a symbol of his journey to the heavenly City. Outside the cathedral he would be aware of the profanity of worldly existence. ('profane' come from two Latin roots meaning 'before the temple'). The strength, grace and inspiring shape of the cathedral would speak to him of prayer and he would be pointed to another and better world by the spire. Above the main west door he would see graphic images of either the Last Judgement, helping him to focus the true ends of life, or sculptured sequences in the life of the Blessed Virgin Mary possibly with the figure of Christ in some commanding position, encouraging him to believe in the divine mercy. As he entered the cathedral he would be aware that he crossed a threshold of consciousness. This would be reflected in all that his eyes would see and especially in the light by which he saw. This light would be that filtered through stained glass. Thus the profane light of this world is broken into joyful and harmonious colours suggestive of heaven.[1]

Near the point of entrance he would find the font, so the start of his physical walk is identical with the start of his Christian life in baptism. In the far distance he would see the high altar or at least a Choir enclosing the high altar, as a secret to be opened to him as he is purified by his advancing walk. The ground plan of the cathedral would be cruciform, reminding him that the Church is the Body of Christ and that he must be conformed to Christ if he is to be worthy to receive the blessed sacrament. The nave through which he walks would remind him of a ship ('nave' comes from a Latin word meaning 'ship'), a womb or a glade of trees, quite possibly all three. In this reminder he would know that he is

---

1. C.f. 'And storied windows richly dight, casting a dim religious light.' Il Penseroso, J. Milton.

safe and nourished. Along the walls the stained glass would describe in orderly sequence the story of salvation as recorded in the Bible, the great feasts of the Church, and the great doctors and saints. His walk is thus an education and an evironing with the community of heaven and divine truth. The walls and vault would be frescoes with floral patterns or figures complementing what the windows contain. Statuary on the string courses of the nave would supplement the sacred themes and include fantastic creatures so brilliantly evoked by St Bernard and included either for their symbolic import, as sports of the fertile creative imagination of the medieval sculptor or as signs of the universal lordship of Christ since it was believed that fantastic creatures inhabited the edges of the world.

At the crossing he would encounter the large rood screen and behold what was seen distantly as soon as he entered the cathedral, a figure of the crucified Jesus, with St John the Evangelist on one side and the Blessed Virgin on the other.[1] Angels might complete the ensemble. On one side at ground level he would find the pulpit and on the other the lectern for the services' book. At this point he would be reminded of the cost to God of his redemption and of the importance of instruction by sermon and liturgy, which included Bible readings.

Passing into the Choir and elevated in doing so by steps, suggestive of the purifying process, he would see before him the resplendent high altar with the beautiful east window behind. This is the inner sanctuary of the Cathedral. Here the monks say their offices and the Mass is celebrated. He would find in the remembrance of monks and priests a reminder of the sacrifice of their lives for God in obedience, poverty and chastity. They would be seen as wise and spiritual counsellors available in case of need. At the high altar he would kneel, finding in the posture humility before the majesty and generosity of God and childlikeness in the receiving of Christ in the blessed sacrament. Somewhere near would be the Lady Chapel and possibly the shrine of a departed saint. He would pray in the one and at the other.

---

1. St John 19.25–27

Joseph Campbell, whose numerous writings on ancient mythologies and religions are very popular in circles where the spiritual is admitted but Christian claims are denied, relates that he visited Chartres Cathedral nine times. He was convinced that the art is anecdotal. This he contrasts with Buddhist art which gives clarity and radiance. Without denying what Buddist art may give, Campbell, as usual, mistakes the Christian vision. Having worked daily in two cathedrals for the space of sixteen years I find the possibility of discovering divine beauty everywhere. It is impossible to describe the stained glass of Chartres as Campbell does, although it relates the Bible story of redemption. The shape of Mary in *La Belle-Verriere*, the rose windows, the colour and harmony of the glass itself, raises the total experience above the anecdotal. Divine beauty is discovered through the anecdote, as Christians say salvation is achieved through history. That this is likely to be true, quite apart from our present experience, is clear from the fact that many of the figures in the stained glass windows cannot be distinguished for distance, and even if they could be, their identity cannot be guessed. The original glass artists knew this but absorbed the fact into a higher aim.

The actual living experience of a great medieval cathedral also enables us to say that the ecclesiastical legitimation of decoration as being educative omits the crucial reality given by the artists through the mysterious manifestation of sacred beauty. Medieval thinking and feeling was exultantly aware of the significance of such beauty. To Suger's understanding of its meaning we may add that of the circumspect and largely Aristotelian St Thomas Aquinas. He separated beauty from goodness and truth and stated that 'beauty requires three things, to wit, first wholeness, for what is impaired is ugly by this very fact; second, a fitting proportion or harmony; third, brightness, for that which has a shining colour is said to be beautiful'. Again, 'beauty ... appeals to the cognitive faculty, for we call beautiful whatever pleases when seen',[1] but the more mystical perception of the Platonic Suger we have already noted.

---

1. Quoted E. Panovsky, *Renaissance and Renascences in Western Art*, p. 184, Icon Edition, 1972

Whatever reverence was granted a church building and its decoration no worship was entailed. The medieval attitude to conservation was quite different from our own. For example, the new Gothic style of the thirteenth century inspired Bishops' Wayneflete and Wykeham totally to re-model the Romanesque nave of Winchester Cathedral and make it one of the most glorious Gothic structures in existence. Duccio's masterpiece, the *Maestà* was completed in 1311 and destined for the Cathedral in Siena. Much pomp and circumstance surrounded its installation, with shops closing for the event and processions accompanying it through the street to the siting. But it replaced a painting known as the Madonna of Grace. It was believed that the Madonna represented in this painting heard the prayers of the Sienese in their battle with the Florentines at Montaperti in 1261. Nevertheless, Duccio's Maestà was 'more beautiful, larger and full of devotion, with scenes of the Old Testament and the New Testament on the back'.[1] It should not surprise us to learn that 'the medieval mason had no qualms about destroying the work of a predecessor, however costly, recent or exquisite, if he felt able to replace it with something more worthy or grandiose'.[2]

THE RENAISSANCE, REFORMATION AND ENLIGHTENMENT

The Renaissance was the period when man and the world were re-discovered. It was a time when Antiquity was newly honoured. It was a time when man began to consult his own reason as well as listen to the voice of corporate authority, whether of Church or state. The stress on individuality included a recognition of the artist as a creator. Previously the artist was considered only a maker. God alone created.

---

1. André Chastel, *Art of the Italian Renaissance*, p. 42, 1988
2. W. Rodwell and J. Bentley, *Our Christian Heritage*, p. 111, George Philip, 1984. This tradition continued through the Renaissance. Thus we find the Lord of Rimini commissioning Alberti (1450) radically to change the shape of the Gothic church of St Francis into a contemporary structure. See H. W. Janson, *History of Art*, p. 469–70, 4th ed. 1991

In the Renaissance man's Godlikeness was asserted. The Renaissance was not inherently anti-religious or anti-Christian, but the accidental forces of history produced a strain between ecclesiastical authority and art which, with the eventual and somewhat different force of the Enlightenment created a rift from which European culture has not yet recovered. Every culture determines the form if not the essence of the art of its time. In the first centuries of the Christian era the pain of man's temporality was deeply felt. The Christian response in art was to see Christ as the conqueror of death. He is portrayed on the cross as strong and with open eyes. In medieval times a deep pessimism and sense of penitence was abroad. Christ on the cross becomes the perfect penitent, sagging, wounded, humiliated. In the Renaissance the dignity of man is re-discovered and Christ is figured as the perfect man. Michaelangelo was a Catholic Christian of evangelical fervour. By 1512 he had completed painting the vault of the Sistine Chapel. This Creation cycle contains a brooding power and colourful humanism, but the rise of Protestantism, the sack of Rome, the Counter-Reformation and the vicissitudes of his own life are all reflected in the troubled force of the Last Judgement painted on the west wall between 1536 and 1541. But he remains a Renaissance painter. Ten figures are naked and Christ is athletic, beardless and youthful. St Catherine was displayed in frontal position and partly nude. And Michaelangelo quite understood the quality of his achievement. St Bartholomew is shown holding a flayed skin with the head of the artist. St Bartholomew is associated by tradition with the Holy Spirit. Michaelangelo was claiming that in spite of the agony God inspired his work.

Such individualism and artistic assertiveness did not please ecclesiastical authority. Some wanted the fresco destroyed. Some wanted it corrected to illustrate Christian modesty. Some tried to persuade Michaelangelo of his mistakes. In 1545 Aretino wrote to the artist, 'Remember that pagans in their statues – I don't say of Diana clothed, but in the naked Venus – made them cover with their hands the parts that should not be revealed; and one who is a Christian, because he values Art more than Faith, displays as a genuine spectacle not only the absence of decorum in the martyrs and virgins, but also the gesture of the man dragged away by his genital organs, a sight to which eyes would be shut tight even in a brothel. What you have done would be appropriate in a voluptuous whore-house, not a supreme choir'.[1] Michaelangelo resisted such appeals. As a Renaissance man he valued truth to nature and was unashamed of the human form, created by God. Power lay, however, with the ecclesiastical hierarchy. The Council of Trent in 1563 commissioned de Volterra to reverse the position of St Catherine and to discreetly cover all evidence of pudenda, despite the protestations of those who cited the 'Song of Songs' and the need of art to be true to nature.

The case involving Paul Veronese (c.1528–88) must also be mentioned. Typical of the golden age of Venetian painting Veronese painted highly coloured feasts and crowd scenes. His *Last Supper* was painted in 1573. The composition included an inner and an outer chamber. Christ and the disciples are within, a crowd is without. Veronsese was summoned before the Inquisition for the irreverence of his work which, it was alleged, included 'a buffoon with a parrot on his wrist … a servant whose nose was bleeding … dwarfs and similar vulgarities'. The authorities were worried among other things by the aspersions concerning the mass levelled by Lutherans. In his defence Veronese replied, 'I received the commission to decorate the picture as I saw fit. It is large and it seemed to me, it could hold many figures.' He added significantly, 'We painters like poets and fools claim license', and he referred to the nudes of Michaelangelo. All to no avail. Veronese was ordered to correct his painting and to pay the legal costs of the hearing! To what extent the artist thought he had lost the argument rather than the power struggle may be gauged by the fact that he archly left the painting as it was and changed the title from *The Last Supper* to *Christ in The House of Levi*.

Influential in the cases of these two artists was the thinking

---

1. André Chastel, *Art of the Italian Renaissance*, pp. 193–4, London, 1988

of the Council of Trent (1545–63), called into being to reform
a partly corrupt Church and to answer Protestant theology.
On the question of images, the long tradition of the Church
was re-affirmed. Images of Christ, the Virgin and other saints
are to be reverenced and honour and veneration are to be
given them. There is no idolatry 'because the honour which
is shown them is referred to the prototypes which those
images represent ... by means of the histories of the
mysteries of our Redemption, portrayed by paintings or
other representations, the people are instructed, and
confirmed in [the habit of] remembering, and continually
revolving in mind the articles of faith'. Abuses and supersti-
tions are to be avoided and bishops must take care 'that
there be nothing seen that is disorderly, or that is unbecoming or confusedly arranged, nothing that is profane,
nothing indecorous, seeing that holiness becometh the
house of God (Psalm 92.5)'[1]. Thus, although the ancient
teaching is re-stated, it is done so in a restrictive manner,
reflective of a defensive cultural atmosphere.

However this may be, in the examples drawn from the
lives of these two artists we see the new forces unleashed by
the Renaissance and the inability of institutional power to
rise to the challenge. Michaelangelo and Paul Veronese were
theologians as well as artists and both were correct in their
painting. It is a repressive puritanism that cannot look upon
human generative organs in the context of a religious painting where a nude would be appropriate. The Last Supper is
the type of the mass, and Catholics in practice have recognised the rightness of the multitude participating in it.
Anglicans remember their midnight eucharists at Christmas.

Veronese's statement likening artists to poets and fools and
thereby claiming license is, in fact, a profound statement,
though he may have made it with a sly smile. After all, who
were the fools in the common sense? More seriously, the
Fool is the type of innocence, of man in paradise before the
fall, of virgin consciousness, before man was separated from

---

1. Transl. J. Waterworth, *The Canons and Decrees of the Sacred and Eucemenical
Council of Trent*, pp. 1233–6, London, 1848

God. In this fallen world institutional authority is necessary, but all too easily it hardens into insensitivity and arrogance. The Fool is a corrective, reminding us of a higher, more happy world. He invites us to put aside our solemnity and burst the bonds of custom. As Cecil Collins so magnificantly wrote, 'The greatest Fool in history was Christ'.[1] We are brought back to the earlier discussion (pp. 7–11) about the significance of prophetic religion set amid the whole pattern of Israelite religion. The prophet and the artist are path-finders, sensitive antenae as to what is actually happening or will happen soon. They are people who seem heretics today and tomorrow are deemed orthodox. We will refer to this point when we speak of sacred visual art in the Church today.

One religious development of the Renaissance was the Reformation. The great Reformers, like the Renaissance scholars, returned to the original texts in their original languages and discovered what they believed to be irreconcilable differences between the New Testament and the contemporary Church. Calvin and Zwingli, out of respect for the Second Commandment and a belief that salvation was by faith, and faith came through hearing the Word, undercut much of the fabric of the Catholic Church. The priest, the sacramental system, the institution itself were all dependent on the preaching of the gospel, through Bible and sermon. The effect of believing this was the virtual denuding of church buildings, a suspicion of art, and an elevation of the sense of hearing above the sense of sight. Luther agreed with much of this, though he considered church ornament an indifferent rather than a pernicious thing. He teaches that, 'God nowhere forbids images other than those of God, as long as they are not adored. Why, he himself raised up and allowed the bronze serpent among that very people until it began to be worshipped ... Paul says to us (1 Cor. 8.4): "We know that an idol is nothing in the world", and all those external things are free, even if they are images assigned to some divine worship.'[2] Compared with the witness of scrip-

1. *The Vision of the Fool and Other Writings*, p. 74, Golgonooza Press, 1994
2. Edited J. Pelikan, *Luther's Works*, vol. 9, p. 81, Concordia Publishing House, 1960

ture Calvin finds St Gregory's view that images are the books of the ignorant to be 'a wicked lie'.[1] Calvin believed that no images were permitted in churches for the first five hundred years of its life and that any image pertaining to God has a fatal tendency to mislead.

Eamon Duffy has traced the effect of such teaching on the visual aspect of religion in England. His book is significantly called *The Stripping of the Altars*. In 1535 Bucer's attack on images was translated into English. The following year Bishop Latimer addressed Convocation attacking the cult of saints, images, lights, relics, holy days, pilgrimages, pardons and purgatory. Images, he declared 'only represent things absent'. In 1536 and 1538 Royal Injunctions were issued attacking most of these things as superstitious and only practised for monetary gain. Other royal orders seemed to contradict this but the Bishops' Book was clear that 'God in his substance cannot by any similitude or image be represented or expressed'.[2] The later King's Book admitted images though no godly honour was to be paid to them. Keith Thomas confirms this general position, relating that 'The Edwardian Reformation saw much iconoclasm and deliberate fouling of holy objects. Mass books, vestments, roods, images and crosses were summarily destroyed. Altar stones were turned into paving stones, bridges, fireplaces, or even kitchen sinks ... Protestantism thus presented itself as a deliberate attempt to take the magical elements out of religion, to eliminate the idea that the rituals of the Church had about them a mechanical efficiency, and to abandon the effort to endow physical objects with supernatural qualities by special formulae of consecration and exorcism. Above all, it diminished the institutional role of the Church as the dispenser of divine grace. The individual stood in direct relationship to God and was solely dependent upon his omnipotence.'[3]

1. *Institutes of the Christian Religion*, Bk 1, ch.xi, sec. 5. Trans. H. Beveridge, James Clarke, 1957
2. Op. cit. p. 442, Yale University Press, 1992
3. *Religion and the Decline of Magic*, pp. 86–7, Peregrine, 1978

The reader may visit the monastic ruins at Glastonbury, Fountains, Rielvaux, Winchester and many other places to see the completeness of the visual devastation (some portions of these derelict sites were removed haphazardly in later times). The reader may visit the Shrine at Walsingham and reflect that it was a waste site until the Anglican re-building of this century. The reader may visit the sites of the shrines at Chichester, Hereford, Canterbury and other cathedrals and feel the gap which witnesses to a massive artistic, devotional and theological destruction. There were 825 religious houses in England before the Reformation, about 100 survived, put to other uses. At Winchester cathedral stained glass in prodigious amount and superb in quality was smashed, about 200 statues, some of them small, were carted away, including the magnificent statuary of the high altar screen. A surviving fragment of that screen of a Madonna and Child, found fortuitously in the nineteenth century, used contemptuously as building stone for a wall, is unsurpassed in artistic and devotional power, tiny reminder of what we have lost. Sir Herbert Read wrote of a thirteenth century torso, perhaps of Fortitude or Ecclesia, that in this Winchester statue 'all the transcendent grace and spirituality of a great religion are embodied in stone'.[1]

The Protestant churches became auditoriums rather than holy theatres, and this applied predominantly within the Church of England until the Catholic Revival in the latter part of the nineteenth century. Stone altars were replaced by holy tables, the pulpit grew in size and was often placed at the east of the nave. Fixed pews developed, row on row facing the pulpit and lectern, places from which the Word sounded. Priestly or ministerial apparel became simple, dignified and largely black. After much debate the Church of England opted for cassock, surplice, academic hood, scarf and stole, depending on the rite being observed. The Roman Catholic church was legally suppressed in England until Catholic Emancipation was finally granted in 1829. While the Baroque style of painting and architecture in Catholic Europe asserted

---

1. *The Meaning of Art*, p. 4, Faber and Faber, 1931

grandiloquently, and sometimes rhetorically, the truth of
Catholicism, in England the Puritan Rebellion devasted
further the visual heritage of the Church and ingrained an
auditory rather than a visual sense in English people. The
Journal of George Fox is instructive in this respect. During
the year 1646 he recounts that 'At another time it was
opened to me that God, who made the world, did not dwell
in temples made with hands. This, at the first, seemed a
strange word, because both priests and people used to call
their temples or churches dreadful places, holy ground, and
the temples of God. But the Lord showed me, so that I did
see clearly, that he did not dwell in these temples which men
had commanded and set up, but in people's hearts'.[1]

If we turn from Fox to the moderate Caroline Divine,
Jeremy Taylor, who represents the classical tradition of
Anglican thought, we find the exhortation to look for godly
likeness in living Christians rather than dead images. He
believes that Roman Catholics worship images but that the
Bible and the early Fathers condemn them, that Simon
Magus began the worship of images, that their worship is a
violation of the Second Commandment, that they offend the
enemies of Christianity and cause Christians to fall into the
sin of idolatry, that it is futile to try and distinguish between
reverence and worship.[2]

The restoration of the Monarchy and the Established
Church in 1660 was followed quickly by the Great Fire of
London in 1666. In Sir Christopher Wren was found an architect of supreme ability. St Paul's Cathedral, begun in 1675
drew its inspiration largely from St Peter's, Rome, Byzantium
and the Baroque. The dome is sometimes thought the finest
in the world, but Wren had the wisdom to employ some of
the best available artists and masons for decoration. Grinling
Gibbons made the fine stalls, organ case and screen behind.
The Frenchman Jean Tijou made various splendid iron-
wrought gates and Cibber, Thornton and Bird all found

1. P.6, London, 1924. In the same passage Fox rejects university trained priests as
unfit, 'an anointing within man' is all
2. *Works*, ed. R. Heber, X, pp. 171–5; XI, p. 157; X, pp. 242–245; X, p. 165–167; X,
pp. 162–3

scope for their talents. It is significant that although Wren wanted a Protestant Cathedral, its basic unit being the square, that could be sub-divided or extended as required, its exterior stone being glistening white Portland, and its glass mainly plain, the decoration he wanted at the east end was rejected by the Dean and Chapter, for betraying Roman influences. It was left to Sir James Richmond (1890) to add the kind of mosaic Wren desired, and Dykes Bower and Godfrey Allen to add a large baldacchino, to Wren's design, above the high altar in 1958.

Wren saw with clearer theological eyes than the Dean and Chapter, but involved in any discussion of the achievement of St Paul's as a Christian church, compared say, with Westminster Abbey is not only the Protestant perception, but that of the Enlightenment. This began in England with the work of Newton, Locke and the rise of science and the experimental habit. So far as sacred visual art was concerned it was mainly a disaster. The concept of reason which, until this time, had included a recognition of intuition as reason's divinest element, assumed a reductionist limitation which philosophers sometimes call technical reason. The Platonic experience of the archetypes grew foreign. Deep feeling was called sentiment or sentimentality. Tradition itself was conceived more as enchaining than supporting man. So much of tradition was thought to have been found false in the cold light of reason. Religious wars and theological quibbles had been found unproductive and the possibility of improving man's lot on earth seemed practical. According to Alexander Pope:

> 'Presume not the Heaven's scan,
> The proper study of mankind is man.'

Thus the stage was set for human self-confidence, mundane concern, and practical activity. Industrialism and technology soon followed man's scientific awakening. Society lost its integration, rational humanism in various guises became the prevailing philosophy, art and religion were diminished, not only in public regard, but in the depth of their own operation.

In line with the prevailing philosophy which saw the universe as a mechanism and man's technical reason as the efficient investigative tool eighteenth century churches were often whitewashed and medieval wall-paintings happily covered if the churches were old. Newly built churches, as in the brilliant work of Hawksmoor, followed in the steps of Wren by being geometric and block-like in form, not growing by aggregation, as was the case with Gothic structures, but by sub-division or by the addition of similar blocks. Glass was preferably plain, reflective of the clear light of reason and when coloured, as in the virtues' windows by Sir Joshua Reynolds in the narthex of New College Chapel, Oxford, they are wholly unconvincing as sacred art. Interior decoration include large, figured memorials and tombs of the gentry, emphasising the class structure, the Royal Arms, emphasising the Monarchy, and the Ten Commandments and Creed or Lord's Prayer on either side of the altar, emphasising the Christian code to be remembered in the absence of much vision to be seen. Protestant chapels and meeting-houses broke with the earlier church tradition by choice. They tended to be preaching houses, with central, prominent pulpit, simple interiors, plain glass, and holy table, either erected when the Lord's Supper was celebrated, or placed diminuatively beneath the pulpit. Fixed pews filled the body of the chapel and colour schemes were modest and purely decorative. A visual eloquence pervades some of these conventicles, but it is of a homely kind, suffused occasionally by an invisible atmosphere.

John Wesley perpetuated the Protestant and Enlightenment perception of sacred images. He believes that the first Christians had no images, that they were introduced with the social acceptance of Christianity partly to do good as the books of the ignorant but that idolatry corrupted their use. A typical entry in his *Journal* reads, 'I once more took a serious walk through the tombs in Westminster Abbey. What heaps of meaningless stone and marble! But there was one tomb that showed common sense. Here indeed the marble seems to speak, and the statues appear only not alive.' [1]

How much of this visual history was inevitable it is difficult to be sure. The secular mind was hardly re-assuring
when we contemplate the massive injuries to visual culture
in France in the wake of the French Revolution, but the
Catholic Church, prior to the Revolution was itself not re-
assuring. J. Gimpel reports that at the Abbey of St Denis, to
make it easy for the dais to be moved in and out of the
church for ceremonial occasions, a pier was removed from
the central doorway and the stone statue of St Denis was
broken. The lintels of three portals and carved columns
representing Old Testament kings and queens, which decorated the embrasures were destroyed. Old tombstones were
ripped out of the Choir and glazed tiles were replaced by
black and white paving stones. Prior Dom Malaret was
mainly responsible for this and only lack of royal money
prevented him moving the tombs of the kings and queens of
France to the crypt. In 1781–2 he employed Borani to white-
wash the whole interior of the abbey, a work Borani had
accomplished already at Tours, Angers and Chartres.

To build a new high altar in the Cathedral of Notre Dame
in Paris, the famous architect Mansart, in 1699 destroyed the
thirteenth century high altar, a rood screen, choir stalls, and
bas-reliefs on the inner enclosure of the ambulatory.
Recumbent statues and mourning figures on old copper or
stone tombs were demolished. The columns of the apse
were covered with marble slabs ornamented with gilded
metal. In 1752 the thirteenth century stained glass in the
Choir was smashed and plain glass with fleur-de-lys borders
was added. In 1771 Souflot, architect of the Pantheon, broke
the statue of Almighty God on the pier of the central door
and the Wise and Foolish Virgins on either side. In the
tympanum he destroyed the Resurrection of the Dead and
the Archangel Michael holding the scales at the Last
Judgement. He whitewashed the whole interior.

At Le Mans Cathedral in the eighteenth century the thirteenth century high altar and other old altars disappeared.

1. *Works of the Revd John Wesley*, vol. 3, p. 160, London 1829, see also vol. 10, pp. 175–7

Two eighteenth century altars were made from the dislodged
rood screen, and the large piers in the apse were covered in
marble stucco. 18–20,000 lbs of copper was sold. An old
antiquarian tried to prevent the Chapter's vandalism but he
was not allowed even to copy inscriptions on the objects, so
they were lost for ever. So grateful was the Chapter for the
leadership shown by the Bishop in this and doubtless other
enterprises that they had a portrait of him painted and hung
in the vestry, with an inscription thanking him for the
improvements he had made[1].

THE VICTORIANS

The Romantic Age redressed the balance of humanness
somewhat after the thin and critical time of the Age of
Reason. Scott, Blake, Coleridge, Wordsworth, Shelley and
Byron were especially important, proving seminal for the
Catholic Revival in the Church of England in the second half
of the century. Disabilities had been removed from Roman
Catholics, and mutual influence became possible. The
Church of England recovered a sense of dignity, ceremonial
and choreography in worship, dignity in the office of priest,
and tradition in the decoration of churches. C. E. Kempe and
Morris and Burne-Jones brought the art of stained glass to
remarkable heights, comparable occasionally to the achievements of medieval times, though in the case of Burne-Jones
vitality in designs was always lacking. Remarkable church
architects, including Pugin, Bodley, Street, Pearson, Scott
and Butterfield, recovered the great tradition in building.
Butterfield's biographer, P. Thompson, summarises his
aesthetic theory as follows: 'the social notions of conve-
nience and distribution of ornament; the concern for "reality"
which led to the display of structure and materials; and the
belief in gothic historicism, gradually shifting from relatively
strict copyism to an ecclecticism governed only by gothic
principles. These doctrines were crucial in the selection of
elements to be composed. But in the process of composition

1. *The Cathedral Builders*, pp. 23–4, Pimlico, 1993

itself, underlying them all, were the governing romantic principles of the picturesque and the sublime. Both followed from the discovery that buildings should be seen, not as isolated objects, but as part of a landscape. But they represented different moods. The picturesque scene would surprise the beholder, evoke his curiosity, through devices such as variety and irregularity, roughness and intimacy. The sublime on the other hand would evoke terror, like a black thunderstorm or a bottomless chasm. Its attributes were the reverse of the picturesque: vastness of height or length, smoothness, obscurity. These two moods were held to be the extremes, so that between them nicely judged, lay beauty. Beauty was thus regarded as essentially a classical concept, against which both the sublime and the picturesque should be understood as romantic reactions.'[1] From some such principles came Nottingham Cathedral (Pugin), All Saints' Church, Margaret Street, London (Butterfield), Truro Cathedral (Pearson) and in Temple Moore, continuing this tradition, All Saints' Church, Basingstoke (1917).

A problem that became acute in Victorian times, due partly to a re-assessment of the medieval achievement, was the distinction between restoration and preservation. The Camden Society, founded in 1839, fostered the study of ecclesiastical art. It published the periodical *The Ecclesiologist*, and in 1846 took the name of the Ecclesiological Society, surviving until 1868. It was one manifestation of the new mood whereby knowledge of Catholic worship, and church architecture were greatly stimulated. Many took the view that an ancient building should be restored to its original state, given a completeness even, it had never had in history. In the name of restoration enormities were committed. Stone that had acquired a particular mellowness through age became angular and clean. At Winchester Cathedral Canon Nott used his own money to begin the reversal of Wayneflete's and Wykeham's work by inserting his idea of the Romanesque window frames in place of the fourteenth century Gothic additions. Men such as Ruskin and

---

1. *William Butterfield*, pp. 305–6, Routledge & Kegan Paul, 1971

Morris were incensed. Morris founded the Society for the
Protection of Ancient Buildings (1877) 'anti-scrape' as he
called it, partly out of exasperation at the proposed restoration of Tewkesbury Abbey by Sir George Gilbert Scott,
whom Morris and Lethaby regarded as destructively
misguided. In the *Manifesto* of the Society, drafted by Morris
himself, we read: 'No doubt within the last fifty years a new
interest, almost like another sense, has arisen in these
ancient monuments of art; and they have become the subject
of one of the most interesting studies ... yet we think that if
the present treatment of them be continued, our descendents
will find them useless for study and chilling to enthusiasm.
We think that those last fifty years of knowledge and attention have done more for their destruction than all the foregoing centuries of revolution, violence and contempt. For
what is left ... we pray them to remember how much is gone
of the religion, thought and manners of time past, never, by
almost universal consent, to be restored; and to consider
whether it be possible to restore those buildings, the living
spirit of which it cannot be too often repeated, was an insep-
arable part of that religion and thought and those past
manners ... we ... call upon those who have to deal with
them to put protection in place of restoration, to stave off
decay by daily care, to prop a perilous wall or mend a leaky
roof by such means as are obviously meant for support or
covering, and show no pretence of other art, and otherwise
to resist all tampering with either the fabric or ornament of
the building as it stands. Thus, and thus only, shall we
escape the reproach of our learning being turned into a
snare to us; thus and thus only, can we protect our ancient
buildings and hand them down instructive and venerable to
those who come after us.' The spirit of these noble words
remains true and was felt to be true by an increasing number
of Morris's fellow Victorians. We shall return to the question
later whether pressed beyond a certain point they too may
not become a snare for the learned.

   Certainly the words of Morris and those who thought like
him fell on listening ears. In 1913 the Government passed
the Ancient Monuments (Consolidation and Amendment)

Act, which brought all ancient buildings within national and local Government control. An ecclesiastical exemption was permitted ancient church buildings, however, on the basis that these are important, not only for heritage but for worship and mission purposes. So far as the Church of England was concerned it was argued that it had operated central oversight of local churches since the thirteenth century by means of Faculty Jurisdiction. Granted present concerns the Church undertook, and was asked to undertake, a review of its own system of oversight to bring it to the standard now expected of secular buildings. The Dibden Committee was duly formed and in its eventual Report recommended that every diocese should have a committee competent to advise on 'architectural, archaeological, historic and artistic aspects of all applications for change, addition or repair of churches'. In 1921 Diocesan Advisory Committees came into existence at the centre of this network, both for reference and advice and to act as the Church's liaison with governmental agencies and national institutions like the Victoria and Albert Museum and the British Museum. Peter Burman, sometime secretary of Council for the Care of Churches (CCC), who in his time did such invaluable work for sacred visual art in churches, said at the Sacred Trusts' Conference in Philadelphia, USA in 1989 that 'our relationship with such bodies remains one of the principle dimensions of our work and we are – in effect – the Church's own Historic Buildings and Monuments Commission, specifically for churches and cathedrals'.

This arrangement, occasionally modified in the light of experience has worked well for parish churches, notwithstanding criticism to which I shall come later. The testimony of Judith Scott, who was Secretary of the CCC/CAC from 1936–71, in a private letter to me (30 July 1994) is significant in illuminating the situation from the position of a highly placed official in the structure of the institutional Church. She writes: 'Efforts to encourage good liturgical and artistic standards could, if pushed too far, result in the spread of a sterile uniformity, adoption of safe solutions which would avoid controversy. This was always a danger. Sanitised good taste my friend John Betjeman called it. But difficult to avoid: after the First [World] War our churches were too often dingey and depressing, as overfull of furniture as the drawing rooms of the period. Much needed to be done to revitalise the setting and presentation of worship. Unfortunately the 30s were the heyday of the church furnishers, firms whose advertising ... attracted very extensive support from the public. They offered everything, plate, vestments, furniture, stained glass etc. Some of it was quite good but much more was mediocre or really bad. The customers, war-weary, and often heart-broken by bereavement – making it all the harder to criticise their schemes.

Also, of course, following the first world war as again after the second, the structural condition of church buildings was generally very poor. Therefore much of the work of DACs had to be concerned with (a) encouraging repair and better maintainance, (b) discouraging bad artistic work in all fields, (c) pioneering new techniques for conservation (medieval glass, stone decay, wall paintings), (d) encouraging donors to look at original work instead of taking the easy option.

Critics now condemn some liturgical trends which brought a measure of decency to many distressing tatty interiors – just as our successors will condemn for aesthetic poverty the changes made in the name of liturgical reform in the past twenty years or so! And then, as now, quite a lot of good work, of artistic and historic value, was destroyed along the way ...

I think it would be no extravagance to say that, by-and-large, the interior furniture and standards of maintenance and general decency of English parish churches compare very favourably with any country in Europe; that is, if you compare the whole (which is my theme) and not some selected examples.'

Miss Scott's views in regard to cathedrals are also perti-nent: 'The situation regarding cathedrals was more fluid. Every Dean and Chapter was a law to itself, having absolute freedom to do what they liked in their building. From time to time public opinion became vocal. It did so in 1952 over some work to stalls and a monument ... The row resounded for months and was sufficiently potent to frighten the Deans and Chapters into making a small concession. They agreed that the Standing Committee [of] the CCC (being at that time a small, non-elected body of people representative of the best in most relevant fields) should appoint a Cathedrals Advisory Committee [CAC]. So reluctant were they, however, to surrender any of their independence that although this move was widely publicised and acclaimed they would only agree to consult it when and if they felt inclined. It was to be totally distinct from the CCC, which was by then a statutory body and tainted by association with the [General] Synod.

Some Chapters consulted often: some never. For the next 40 years we struggled to persuade them that nemesis would overtake in the end and that they had better make terms accepted by them, and by their critics, or else – Mandatory control did not in fact come until the Care of Cathedrals measure in 1990.'

That Miss Scott, the CCC and later the CAC had something to struggle about is clear from the example of Salisbury Cathedral.[1] This amazing Gothic structure suffered first in modern times from the architect and restorer, James Wyatt (1746–1813) nicknamed 'the destroyer'. Salisbury was only one of his many concerns but there he 'gutted the medieval building'.[2] The thirteenth century choir screen was removed and two chantries demolished. A new choir screen was made from this material. What remained of the ancient glass was removed. The eastern vaulting was lime washed, covering medieval wall paintings.

G. G. Scott swept away Wyatt's screen and put in a metal one, designed by himself and made by Skidmore. Scott also inserted quantities of Victorian stained glass. In our century the Skidmore screen was removed and apparently destroyed in 1959 and in the Chapter House Strong reports that a Canon was responsible for having removed two of the Victorian windows and inserting plain glass. One window has been inserted with imitation Victorian glass.

---

1. See Roy Spring, *Salisbury Cathedral*, pp. 22, Unwin Hayman, 1987
2. Op. cit. p. 22

Until the labours of Walter Hussey from the period of the
Second World War it is the argument of this book that the
Church and the visual arts had ceased to exist in any
symbiotic relationship. The period of the Renaissance, and in
Catholic countries happily into Baroque times with splendid
works by Rubens, Jordaens and El Greco, marked the
progressive parting of the ways. Protestantism devalued the
arts, and especially the visual arts in the service of God.
Rembrandt was one of the most accomplished and profound
Christian painters to have lived, but no canvas of his is
displayed in a church. By the time we come to the twentieth
century there is estrangement. The break with historicism
and the academic tradition occasioned by the Impressionists,
Post-Impressionists, Fauvists, Cubists and all who followed
them, seemed to have left the Church stranded. An educational system with little emphasis on the visual arts and an
incipient Protestantism rendered the Anglican clergy unable
to respond easily to the radical movements in visual art. The
Victorian tradition, continued in the workshop of Kempe,
was valued so that if we place a pin on any spot of a map of
England and draw a radius of thirty miles around it, we
will find a Kempe window within that circle. The figurative
statuary of sculptors unknown in the art world could find a
place, textiles came generally from ecclesiastical furnishers
or were of congregational inspiration. Even with the massive
scheme of embroidery undertaken in Winchester Cathedral
whilst of good craftsmanship standard and though visited
and praised by Queen Mary, it showed in its inconography
no relationship with the contemporary world of the arts and
crafts.

It might be said that visual artists of good or brilliant worth
had turned away from the Church, identifying it with reac-
tion and a fictional transcendentalism. But we may doubt
how completely this view can be sustained. The truth would
seem to be that the Church lived predominantly from within
its own cultural heritage, misunderstood the nature of
modern art, gave limited value to the endeavour of artists
and did not know how to befriend and commission them.
The case of Epstein has been mentioned, but that of David

Jones and Stanley Spencer can be added. Spencer hoped that his deeply felt *Christ in the Wilderness* series of paintings might find their place in a church, but they languished until being sold to an Australian art museum. The Burghclere Memorial Chapel decoration hardly counts as a normal ecclesiastical commission. William Roberts and Edward Burra painted memorable religious paintings, these and others might easily have been drawn into the service of the Church. Eric Gill did work for the Church. An apologist for the Roman Catholic Church, a man who observed the Dominican daily Offices, one who revived a Catholic community of artists and craftsmen, should have been overwhelmed by commissions. Such is not the case. His lettering was in moderate demand, but his sculpture was not. It seems that his excellent Stations of the Cross in Westminster Cathedral came to him as a commission almost by default. The Administrator, frustrated by the architect, informed him that unless he commissioned a sculptor immediately, the commissioning would be done by the Administrator. Understandably, this prompted the architect to take action, and his junior assistant, Eric Gill, was given the work. To complete the story of the recurrent incomprehension by Church authority, when Gill carved a relief of St Thomas More for the chapel dedicated to the saint in this same cathedral, he put a monkey by More's feet, it is being known that St Thomas loved such creatures. This impious image had to be erased!

Whilst the cultural thrust of the times has had something to do with the estrangement between sacred visual art and the Church, blame must lie with the Church, both in clinging to an outdated theology and being unwilling to venture into an aspect of cultural life where once it claimed authority and admiration.

This criticism is strengthened when we compare the fate of music in the service of the Church. Music had not seemed to medieval or Protestant puritans as irrelevant or seductive as visual art, but it is art and it had claimed an autonomy, much as visual art had done during the period from the Renaissance to the Enlightenment. But because music was somehow recognised, especially in cathedrals, as an important support for worship we find new organs entering cathedrals in the course of the nineteenth century, choirs being revived by the enthusiasm and brilliance of such organists and choir masters as S. S. Wesley (1810–76), and the secretary of the Royal Commission on Cathedrals writing to every precentor and organist of the Cathedral and Collegiate churches in England and Wales in 1853 to discover their views on the condition and improvement of music in the service of the Church. In the course of the twentieth century we find many of the most distinguished musicians have composed music for the Church: Elgar, Vaughan Williams, Holst, Fauré, Britten, Stravinsky, Messaien, Tavener, to name some. It is significant that these musicians have composed in the idiom natural to them, and it is common knowledge that a cathedral Evensong may include composers as different in style as Stanford, Bach and Tavener. Music is doubtless less permanent and more abstract than a painting or sculpture, but the popular enthusiasm for church music suggests that sacred visual art might enter again the service of the Church more powerfully if its importance could actually be realised.

If the culture of significant patronage of visual art has waned we find in this century and country individuals and enterprises that have recognised the importance of visual art and have been adventurous in commissioning. I shall mention some of these.

Fr Bernard Walke was born in Wiltshire, the son of a clergyman. He was trained for the priesthood at Chichester Theological College and embraced an Anglo-Catholic ecclesiology that looked forward to re-union with Rome His ministry was spent in Cornwall and his claim to fame rested upon his incumbency at St Hilary, 1913–36. He was a man of independent mind and passionate beliefs. Not only was he prepared to change radically the form and decoration of his church, making it Catholic in a largely Protestant environment, he was a pacifist in the First World War, making no secret of his view, and he preached and taught

Christian Communism in the years after the war wherever there was a platform in Cornwall. He was no bigot and befriended people of diverse beliefs or none.

In his fascinating autobiography, *Twenty years at St Hilary*, Walke described the church as he first found it. 'Within the church was full of pious distractions: a Holy, Holy Holy on red baize decked an altar too small for the proportions of the building; the walls were disfigured with stensil texts; the Lady Chapel was blocked with an organ and the chapel on the opposite aisle crowded with pews.' He proceeds, 'The Catholic Church has always taught the world apprehended by our senses is capable of bringing us into relationship with another world'.[1]

He set about the re-ordering of the church's interior. In the Roman Forum, years before, he had seen a pagan altar, perfect in form, and that was his ideal for the high altar at St Hilary's. It was shaped in granite and soon put in place. He believed that in medieval times local artists and craftsmen were employed in the local churches and he revived this custom. The front of the choir stalls were decorated first depicting the lives of Cornish saints. His own wife, who was a painter, and some Newlyn artists were employed, including Harold Knight, Ernest and Dod Procter, Harold Harvey, Norman and Alathea Garstin and Gladys Hynes. Two chapels were recreated on either side of the high altar, a Lady Chapel and Chapel of the Sacred Heart. Ernest Procter painted a Visitation for the first and a Quentin Matsys (so identified by Roger Fry) from the collection of Walke adorned the second. Ernest Procter painted a Deposition to hang above the altar of the All Souls' Chapel. Two altar pieces were to be found along the aisles of the nave and Annie Walke, his wife, painted a St Joan of Arc for one and Roger Fry painted a St Francis of Assisi for the other. Fry and Walke had lunched together in London and Fry had spent the time attacking Catholicism. As they rose to leave the table he offered to make the painting. Walke was able to buy two sculptured heads from an antique dealer in London from

1. Op. cit., p. 5, London, 1982

money received from the BBC for broadcasting various plays
at St Hilary's, one of them written by Walke himself. One was
an early French Gothic St Anne and the other was a seventeenth century Spanish St Joseph. They were placed in the
Chapel of the Sacred Heart. Joan Manning-Sanders was
persuaded to become a professional painter when Walke
asked her to paint scenes from the Childhood of Jesus for the
screen of the Lady Chapel.[1]

In 1932 the decoration of the church was attacked by
Kensitites, an extreme Protestant group violently hostile to
Roman Catholicism. The cause of the attack may simply have
been the perception of Walke as a Romaniser, but he had
refused to remove a tabernacle erected without permission
and a woman objector may have been present with the
wreckers. Walke, who was held captive in the church as forty
or fifty men vandalised it behaved with dignity and was
allowed to remove the Blessed Sacrament. He contrasted the
violent emotion and sound from within the church with the
peace of walking with the Blessed Sacrament from the
church to the vicarage, people, forewarned, standing or
kneeling as he passed. This anecdote reveals the purpose of
all Walke's striving. It was this same person who had
strangely affected Roger Fry. Later, artist friends came to his
help and, as far as could be, the decoration was re-instated.[2]

Bishop George Bell was Bishop of Chichester from 1929
until 1958. He was perhaps, the most important Anglican
bishop of the century, and among his many concerns lay a
passionate and intelligent understanding of the arts in the
service of the Church. This concern found expression when
he was Dean of Canterbury, especially in the commissioning
of splendid music and drama. Professor E. W. Tristram was
carefully chosen to do restorative work on medieval paintings in the Cathedral. In 1929 Bell was appointed Bishop of
Chichester and said in his enthronement address, 'Whether it

1. Op. cit. pp. 122–135
2. Op. cit. pp. 292–303

be music or painting or drama, sculpture or architecture or any other form of art, there is an instinctive sympathy between all of these and the worship of God. Nor should the Church be afraid to ask the poet and the artists for their help, or to offer its blessing to the works so pure and lovely in which they seek to express the Eternal Spirit. Therefore I earnestly hope that in this diocese (and in others) we may seek ways and means for a reassociation of the Artist and the Church: learning from him as well as giving to him: and considering with his help our conception alike of the character of Christian worship and of the forms in which the Christian teaching may be proclaimed.'[1]

Bell's involvement with and stimulation of John Masefield, Dorothy Sayers, T. S. Eliot, Christopher Fry, Gustav Holst and Charles Williams found no match in the visual artists whom he commissioned and encouraged, though the enthusiasm and care were the same. Along with Sir Herbert Baker in the refurbishment of St Martin's Chapel at Canterbury, he had commissioned Mrs Monnington to paint St Martin and said that the painting was 'one of the most lovely, delicate, and deeply felt modern religious paintings that I know'.[2] At St Elizabeth's, Eastbourne, he enabled Professor Tristram to paint a series of life-sized paintings in 1938. Shortly afterwards he was instrumental in engaging Hans Feibusch, the muralist, to paint the Nativity of Our Lord, in St Wilfrid's Church, Brighton. Bell fully supported the view of the CCC that in the time of war the physical care of local churches and their decoration should not be forfeited. With the cooperation of the Central Institute of Art and Design he arranged a competition for mural painting and, out of the ten artists asked to submit designs, Augustus Lunn was commissioned to paint The Great Commission for Sir Edward Maufe's fine new Bishop Hannington Memorial Church in Hove.

Bishop Bell created at this time the Sussex Churches Art Council, hoping thereby to bring artists of all kinds into connexion with the needs of the Church. In conjunction with

---

1. R. C. D. Jasper, *George Bell, Bishop of Chichester*, p. 121, OUP, 1967
2. Op. cit. p. 129

this Bell initiated a 'Pictures in Churches Loan Scheme' through which paintings by contemporary artists were lent to churches for a month at a time. In his introduction to the catalogue Bell pleaded for today's artists to be employed to paint in our churches not in a style imitative of the past but in the idiom natural to them. He believed the Church had taken 'too narrow a view' of what was appropriate. In 1944 Bell gathered together a group of poets and artists in conference for three days at Chichester. The gathering included T. S. Eliot, Dorothy Sayers, Hans Feibusch, Henry Moore, Edward Maufe, Charles Wheeler and Fr Martin D'Arcy. It was agreed that the Church should use artists fearlessly. An artist need not be a Christian in order to be employed by the Church. The Church should dictate the subject-matter whilst the artist should decide the style. Due regard should be paid to what congregations would accept.

Bell was instrumental in securing permission for Marguerite Thompson to paint a Resurrection in the Chapel at Bishop Otter College, Chichester. The artist had enthused over Stanley Spencer's Resurrection and her conversations with Bell had led to the commission. As the painting proceeded and no central figure of the resurrected Jesus appeared Bell expressed his doubts and concern. At the point of the artist suffering a nervous breakdown and affirming, 'I would rather be burned a heretic than as a bad artist', Bell relented and supported the artist in being true to her vision. An interesting footnote, overlooked by Jasper, is that Spencer's Resurrections are centred usually on the resurrection of Man. It is very likely that this was expressed by the artist, but that Bell misunderstood her and had no proper knowledge of the work of Spencer, one of the greatest English artists of the time and a man of deep, if eccentric, Christian conviction.

In 1953 the Vicar of Goring and his Parochial Church Council (PCC) took advantage of a scheme initiated by Bell to encourage mural paintings in churches. The Sussex Churches Art Council would provide a grant so long as the Council approved the artist. The church proferred Hans Feibusch and a design for Christ in Glory over the Chancel arch. The DAC disapproved the design, finding it too vague. A revised design was submitted and again rejected. The Chancellor decided to hear the case once more, this time in the Consistory Court. The Vicar had expert artistic opinion to support his application, including Mr Philip James, Director of Art for the Arts Council of Great Britain. Exception was taken to the 'violently masculine figure, almost brutal' of Christ. The Chancellor decided to defer judgement and refer to Bell. Bell was able to re-convene the Court and take the chair himself. The Bishop's judgement was historic. He referred to the legal and advisory apparatus surrounding the commissioning of new work in churches as 'concerned primarily with protective and not creative action'.[1] Craftsmen usually have been employed by the Church since they could be controlled more easily than artists. Furthermore, in a legal court a legal point of view was likely to prevail, and exactness in drawings would be looked for. But artists must be left free in designing works for the glory of God. He commented on the process of artistic creation as including change between inception and finish and concluded: 'Unless the Church is to be sterile in the fostering of creative art, it must be prepared to trust its chosen artists to begin their work and carry it through to the end as the fulfilment of a trust, the terms and circumstances of which they understand and respect'.[2]

Jasper makes no mention of an important mural and painting project for Berwick Church. It began with a suggestion to Bell by Sir Charles Reilly, sometime professor of architecture at Liverpool University. Bell took up the suggestion and was writing to Reilly in 1941 that Duncan Grant, Vanessa Bell, and her son and daughter would cooperate on a grand scheme for the little church. Duncan Grant was to paint a Christ in Glory for the chancel arch, Vanessa Bell an Annunciation and Nativity for the north and south sides of the nave, Quentin Bell was to paint a Wise and Foolish Virgins for the east side of the chancel arch and Angelica Bell

1. Jasper, op. cit. p. 132
2. Jasper, op. cit. p. 133

was to decorate the south aisle wall. Additions included the painting of the screen and pulpit, a Crucifixion by Duncan Grant on the west wall, an altar piece by Quentin Bell and an altar cloth with a Virgin and Child. Richard Shone, who tells the story, speaks of the 'seemingly endless labyrinth of setbacks and church politics'.[1] The PCC approved the project by a majority. The first meeting of the DAC was disappointing. A village meeting was called with Bell, Grant and others supporting the project present. It was a depressing occasion. The DAC met again and Sir Kenneth Clark and the President of the local Archaeological Society spoke in favour. The Chancellor approved the petition and the work went ahead. Clark wrote to Bell that Vanessa Bell's panels 'seem to be amongst the very best things she has ever done ... All things considered I believe that these decorations will remain a fine monument to English painting of this period and a complete justification of your experiment'. According to Sir John Rothenstein 'they must, I think, be accounted among the best paintings to be made in church or chapel in England during the present century'. The pictures were dedicated in 1943, and their number was modestly added to in the years following. A footnote to this brave venture was a commissioning of Duncan Grant to decorate the Russel Chantry in Lincoln Cathedral. This was completed in 1958. Christ the Good Shepherd among sheep and shepherds dominates the east wall. Good artists as Vanessa Bell and Grant were it may be questioned whether their perception of life allowed them to rise to the height of commissions in sacred art.

In 1948 Bell held a visitation in the Cathedral. In the course of a prophetic statement about the ministry cathedrals might undertake he said that residentiary canons should be given specific briefs involving them in diocesan work. The Treasurer, for example, might revive his earlier role of care for the treasures of the Cathedral and be a kind of minister of religious artists and craftsmen in the services of the Church.[2]

1. *The Berwick Church Paintings*, Towner Art Gallery, 1969
2. Jasper, op. cit., p. 358

Curiously omitted by Jasper was one of Bell's final acts, a strong commendation of Walter Hussey as the new Dean of Chichester. Hussey had become famous but controversial in commissioning poetry, music and visual art for St Matthew's Church, Northampton, by distinguished non-ecclesiastical artists. Bell's sponsorship of Hussey elevated the cause of art in the Church as its best contemporary champion was going into retirement.

Walter Hussey. According to Sir Kenneth Clark Hussey's work at St Matthew's, Northampton broke a threshold that had been virtually sealed since the Earl of Shrewsbury supported Pugin in the mid-nineteenth century.[1] With little clear guidance or encouragement this son of a clergyman, unlikely ever to marry, had found his way to music and the visual arts. As a curate in London he frequented the art galleries and museums. Despite the modernism attached to his name he once confided to me that he regarded the medieval achievement as the greatest. He stood out in any company by dint of his remarkable head, with its large, intelligent forehead, and quick warm eyes. A man of contrasts, he could be cold and proud, but he had an innate ability to respond to visual and auditory beauty.

He read very little theology and his earlier Anglo-Catholicism melted into an ecclesiastical liberalism, with a distaste for St Paul and conventicle-type Christianity. His capacious mind was largely intuitive and he came to rapid conclusions, often correct, without always knowing the reasoned steps leading to the conviction. No great lover of the human race he had a deceptive charm and a forgiving spirit.

From the outset of his commissioning work he understood what to do. He applied to the best artist and if there seemed no one adequate he would wait. He had his own views about artists and would ask a few trusted connoisseurs for confirmation or suggestions. Kenneth Clark and Henry

1. Dean Walter Hussey – A Tribute to his Patronage to the Arts, *Chichester 900*, p. 68, 1975

Moore acted in this role. He understood also that the local church must be prepared to stand with him in any commissioning venture, and so he prepared the PCC carefully, and artists might visit the church and speak with parishioners. In the conviction that he had secured the right artist for the appropriate commission and the local people stood with him, he faced the rowdy world with equanimity.

Moore's Madonna and Child was unveiled in St Matthew's in 1944. He was attracted to Moore by seeing his war-time drawing of sleepers in the Underground. He was encouraged in his enterprise by Clark, who wrote of Moore, 'I consider him the greatest living sculptor and it is of the utmost importance that the Church should employ artists of first-rate talent instead of the mediocrities usually employed ... his sketches promise that this will be one of his finest works. I am sure that it will shed great lustre on your church'.[1] In their correspondence Moore reflected on the difference between secular and religious art: 'It's not easy to describe in words what this difference is, except by saying in general terms that the "Madonna and Child" should have in austerity and a nobility and some touch of grandeur (even hieratic aloofness) which is missing in the "everyday" Mother and Child idea'.[2]

Rather more than life-size the sculpture is placed in the north nave aisle. Mary looks down the aisle greeting the approaching visitor. The Child Jesus is encountered fully only when the visitor stands abreast the sculpture. Tom Driberg wrote that it had 'something primaeval and eternal: it is hieratic yet human; it has intense dignity, and its beauty grows on you the longer you look at it'.[3] Sir Alfred Munning, President of the Royal Academy, disliked modernism and singled out Moore's sculpture for particular abuse in his Presidential address to the Academy in 1949. Sound and Fury, as Hussey termed it, raged in the media for weeks.

The second great St Matthew's commission was Graham Sutherland's Crucifixion, dedicated in 1946. Hussey had

1. Walter Hussey, *Patron of Art*, p. 30, Weidenfeld and Nicholson, 1985
2. Op. cit. p. 33
3. Op. cit. p. 47

prepared his PCC for the commission by reading some preg-
nant words of Feibusch: 'Let churches be decorated by such
men as Rouault or Graham Sutherland, in whom there is fire
... To see the way some of our best church and cathedral
builders decorate their work with nursery emblems, golden
stars, chubby Christmas angels, lilies, lambs and shepherds,
insipid sculptures and paintings of a silly, false naivety, one
wonders in what world we live. The men who come home
from the war, and all the rest of us, have seen too much
horror and evil ... Only the most profound, tragic, moving,
sublime vision can redeem us.'[1]

Malcolm Yorke has suggested that the religious paintings
of Sutherland came from no special conviction, but were
simply commissions he was prepared to fulfil.[2] But Sutherland was a communicant member of the Roman Catholic
Church, even his non-liturgical painting carry symbols of a
transforming and religious significance, and all his Crucifixion paintings convey the authority of heart-felt belief.
Sutherland had seen photographs of the concentration
camps, he had lived through the war himself and only as he
went back in the tradition of Crucifixion painting to El Greco
and particularly Grünewald did he find the iconography to
release his painting. He fulfilled the hopes expressed in
Feibusch's writing and whilst Bacon could only paint
damned creatures at the foot of the Cross, Sutherland could
find in Christ a symbol to embrace the unspeakable horror of
modern war.

At Chichester Hussey commissioned Sutherland to paint a
Noli me Tangere (1961) for the St Mary Magdalen Chapel,
Geoffrey Clarke making the bronze altar-rails, free-standing
candlesticks and altar book rest and Robert Potter, the
Cathedral Architect, supervising the work and designing the
altar. Hussey declared that his intention was to supply a need
in the Cathedral, not to find expression for his innovative
desires. The Piper High Altar tapestry followed in 1966,
its brilliant colours relieving the dull and undistinguished

1. Op. cit. pp. 54–5
2. *The Spirit of Place*: Nine Neo-Romantic Artists in Their Times, Constable, 1988

sanctuary. Piper explained the semi-abstract iconography as follows: 'The scheme is the Trinity (three central panels) represented by an equilateral triangle among flames, and related to this, symbols of the Father (a white light), the Son (a Tau Cross), and the Holy Spirit (a flame-like wing); and the Evangelists below them – St Matthew (winged man), St Mark (winged lion), St Luke (winged ox) and St John (winged eagle).'[1] Before the tapestry was made by the Pinton Frères, at Felletin, near Aubusson in France an interesting discussion on the iconography took place in which the Archdeacon of Chichester correctly maintained that the triangle could represent the Trinity, but not God the Father. Inspiration from Grünewald's Resurrection painting enabled Piper to introduce the white circle.

Cecil Collins's Icon of Divine Light was placed on the front of the altar in St Clement's Chapel in 1973. Painted on board in gold and yellow colours it displays the sun amid stars, or sun-flower in a paradisal garden. The sun or flower has a sacred face. Neither Hussey's professional autobiography nor the Pitkin Guide mention this commission. It had been suggested to Hussey by the husband of an artist, Muriel Cox, who had much admired Collins's work before she died. Even so, Hussey saw the commission through and bears responsibility for it. It is possible that he was concerned about the universalist implications of the symbolism or that he rated Collins's artistic merit lower than that of Piper, Sutherland and Moore. If any of these reasons were his I believe him to be wrong. The piece is perfectly consonant with Christian perception, the sun being a traditional symbol of Deity, and it seems to me to have been beautifully painted. It is prophetic of the future and guardians of institutions can find this difficult.

Hussey's final act of patronage was the Arts to the Glory of God window, unveiled in 1978, designed by Marc Chagall and made by Charles Marq. Chagall used the imagery of Psalm 150 for the design and the wonderful reds, blues and greens of the glass beautifully interpret the meaning of the

1. Chichester Cathedral, Pitkin *Visitor's Guide*, 1971

psalm. Only at Tudeley and Stirchely do we find other examples in England of Chagall's stained glass window design prolific and master sacred artist though he was.

Hussey had hoped that Barbara Hepworth might produce metal work for the new West Door of the Cathedral, but she became ill and could not perform the task. He had high hopes also that Henry Moore would produce a Crucifixion and Hussey told me that they had even decided the place where it would stand. This too remained an unrealised dream.

Coventry Cathedral. The new cathedral was dedicated in 1962, rising from the ashes of and making architectural connexions with the old fourteenth century cathedral destroyed by fire bombs in 1940, during the longest air-raid on a British city in the course of the Second World War. The design for the new cathedral was won in open competition by Basil Spence, after a previous design by Giles Gilbert Scott in traditional style had been rejected by the Royal Fine Art Commission. Spence won an open competition between 219 entrants. His creation took into account the need to employ the best artists in the service of the Church, the devotional and social need for reconciliation between enemies, the importance for the Church of being open to the world, the significance of ecumenism in witnessing to one expression of human unity, and the relating of architecture and church decoration to liturgical requirements.

Gone is the triumphalism of the traditional form of cathedrals, gone even the notion of the Church as the centre of the community. The new building is part of the general architectural landscape, built in pleasing tawny sandstone, the emphasis on the Church as the friend and the servant of humanity. We enter the Cathedral at the south west end, passing an external bronze sculpture by Epstein of St Michael conquering the devil. On our left, integrated with the new structure, are the ruins of the old. We enter the main body of the new Cathedral through a door in a glass screen decorated by John Hutton's engraved glass angels and saints.

Thus a link is forged between liturgical and worldly space, a transparent screen alone dividing worshippers and those who may be simply passing by.

The whole nave is dominated by the tapestry, designed by Graham Sutherland, weighing almost a ton and the largest in the world. Like the Piper tapestry at Chichester it was woven by the Pinton Frères, at Felletin, near Aubusson, France. It was given by a resident of Coventry, showing the local sympathy for the remarkable new enterprise of the Cathedral building. It depicts Christ in Majesty. The Byzantine-type face of Christ is strong and compassionate, the eyes following the visitors, wherever they move. The wounded hands and feet are in evidence and just outside the mandorla are the traditional configurations of the four evangelists, thought by Spence never to have been more beautifully depicted. St Michael conquering the devil appears between the eagle and the lion, and the serpent dying in the chalice (St John) appears beneath the feet of Christ. At the base of the tapestry is a crucifixion with angels, which acts as a reredos for the Lady Chapel, which is thus open to the whole church.

As we begin to walk through the nave we are aware of the canopy made of slatted spruce, honey-combing it between concrete beams. On the south side of the nave is the large 200 light baptistry window, designed by John Piper and made by Patrick Reyntiens. The composition of this abstract design manifests the light of the Holy Spirit breaking through the cross currents and conflicts of the world. At its foot in stark contrast to the sumptuous light above is an unworked boulder taken from a hillside just outside Bethlehem and serving as the font. Opposite is the Chapel of Unity, created by, paid for, and used by different nationalities and denominations. Einar Forseth of Sweden created the floor mosaic.

Stone tablets decorate the walls of the nave with biblical texts carved by Ralph Beyer of Germany. There are ten nave stained glass windows, each some 21 metres (70 feet) high. They lie in the folds of the nave walls, so that they are invisible as we approach the altar, but glorious in colour and design as we look west down the nave, usually as a worshipper turns after receiving communion. The colours and design fortify the same symbolic reality, green for the begin-nings of natural world and human life, red for the interven-tion of God in the world and man in history and time, blue and purple for maturity and suffering, silver and gold for the vision of God's Kingdom. The dramatic Chapel of Christ in Gethsemane is entered by the grille composed as a metal crown of thorns by Spence and on the wall opposite and made by Stephen Sykes is a large angel holding a chalice. Sleeping apostles are depicted in mosaic on the wall adjacent to the angel. The Chapel is made to admit maximum light. It is a focal point for all who enter the Cathedral and an invitation to prayer.

Just before the official consecration Yehudi Menuhin came into the newly created Cathedral with his violin. Quite spon-taneously he began to play Bach. At the consecration service Spence and some of his assistants wept. The thrill and cost of achieving sacred art are things for us all to cherish.

If the decoration of the Liverpool Anglican Cathedral had been better than it is it would have been included in this brief list of individual ecclesiastical commissioning. John Betjeman has said well, 'This is one of the great buildings of the world ... the impression of vastness, strength and height no words can describe ... suddenly, one sees that the greatest art of architecture, that lifts one up and turns one into a king, yet compels reverence, is the art of enclosing space'.[1] Begun in 1904, the twenty two year old Giles Gilbert Scott won the open competition among 123 competitors. It is significant that Scott frequently changed the design in large and small parts. Happily, the Cathedral authorities let him have his way, understanding that creativity cannot be closely bound. How would Scott fare with today's regulations? The surprising citation by the Royal Institute of British Architects on the occasion of their award to the Cathedral on its completion and made in 1979 leaves us in no doubt how professionals regarded Scott, 'a major Cathedral of interna-tional rank ... The overwhelming achievement this building represents is worthy of the highest merit, and this is so,

---

1. *Liverpool Cathedral*, p. 5, Fine Art Publications

regardless of time'.[1] Apart from the stained glass by Carl
Edwards and the form but not the decoration of the font
there is little to arrest the eye on a journey through this
magnificent building.

The Metropolitan Cathedral of Christ the King, Liverpool.

Scott was a Roman Catholic who designed an Anglican
Cathedral, Frederick Gibberd was an Anglican who designed
a Roman Catholic Cathedral. Gibberd was lucky in being
able to absorb the new liturgical thinking, expressed in
Vatican II in the building. The Council determined that priest
and people, in the mass, should not be separated. Dialogue
must be real. Gibberd chose in consequence a circular form
for the new Cathedral, and work began in 1962. The main
axis is north south, with the Blessed Sacrament Chapel
beyond the central high altar and in direct line with the main
south entrance on the opposite side. The dark grey marble of
the floor is extended almost throughout the Cathedral to
encourage the perception of one equal space in the sacred
area of the Cathedral. The great lantern tower, which weighs
2,000 tons, is one of the building's glories. It is functionally
related to the main space as a light illuminating the high
altar, above which it rises. Light pours into the building
through it by day, and by night it is lit so as to radiate out
over the city. Seen from a distance it looks like the crown of
a king. John Piper made the design for the lantern and
Patrick Reyntiens created the glass. Abstract in design it
symbolises the Trinity, the unity of the Godhead indicated by
a spectrum of colours and the Three Persons differentiated
by differing white lights. The massive and plain high altar is
surmounted by a remarkable metal crucifix made by
Elisabeth Frink, who also made the lectern eagle as a young
sculptor for Coventry Cathedral. Piper and Reyntiens made
the stained glass for the Chapel of St George and the
English Martyrs and Ceri Richards designed the windows, the

1. Op. cit. p. 15

tabernacle and created the painting above the altar, in the Blessed Sacrament Chapel.

If readers of these pages were to visit in turn today St Matthew's Northampton, Chichester Cathedral, Liverpool Anglican and Roman Catholic Cathedrals and Coventry Cathedral, they will not only marvel at particular points of artistic and sacred excellence, they will recognise sadly in each of these places that the practice of excellence has not been maintained since the period covered in these pages: the addition of Malcolm Pollard's sculpture of the Risen Christ at St Matthew's, of an expressionistic and relentless tapestry at the site of the shrine of St Richard in Chichester Cathedral by Ursula Benker-Schirmer, (Walter Hussey gave his assent to a design by Cecil Collins, commissioned by me, illustrated in W. Anderson's *Cecil Collins*[1], which, with his retirement was rejected by Chapter), of white illuminated ship sails that change colour on the hour in the Liverpool Anglican Cathedral, of textiles added in recent years and a questionable choice for the design and creation of Stations of the Cross at the Liverpool Roman Catholic Cathedral, and most items added in Coventry Cathedral. This strengthens the conviction of these pages that good commissioning is no longer a cultural, but only an individual, possibility in our time. It also gives point to some important words by Judith Scott, appended to the letter to myself quoted earlier: 'You asked what I thought of the present state of the Church and the Arts. My feeling is that some Deans and Provosts are too anxious to make a personal impact on the Cathedral of which they are the temporary custodians. They may often seem to seek originality at the expense of congruity. In other words paying too little attention to the pre-eminent totality of the building itself. In doing so they sometimes appear to forget that though it may be good to challenge visitors with some fresh presentation of the Faith, in so doing they damage the atmosphere of peace and harmony which means much to regular worshippers as well as to many visitors. The same may be said of some

1. P. 159, London, 1988

parochial clergy, though they have less money to lavish on fashionable gimmickry.'

Before leaving this chapter we must salute the French achievement during the same period. The extraordinary flowering of sacred art in the time of the Second World War and immediately afterwards in a few French churches had deep roots that have not been investigated historically as they deserve. For example, the Beuron school was an influential community of religious painting centred on the South German Benedictine Abbey of Beuron. The school was founded by Didler Lenz with the aim of evolving an art comparable with plain song and based on a canon of sacred measurements inspired by those of ancient Egypt. Their principal work can be found in the mother Abbey at Monte Casino, Italy, made during the years 1877–1910. Through Denis and Serusier, members of the Nabis, this German influence helped to form *Art Sacré*. Emile Bonnard was influenced by this whole development. Les Nabis were a group of French artists formed in 1888 under the impact of Gaugin's pont-aven paintings. Pierre Bonnard, Eduard Vuillard, Denis Serusier and Maillol were members. The word 'nabi' is Hebrew for 'prophet' and mystical perception was important for them. The work and influence of both these groups affected ateliers d'art sacré which were started by Desvalliéres in 1919. In 1935 the magazine *L'Art Sacré* began.

Pre-eminent among those associated with the magazine and the philosophy it advocated was the Dominican priest, who had once been a painter, Fr Marie-Alain Couturier. Due to his courage, persistence and discriminating perception splendid work was won for the Church. The little church at Assy is today visited by hosts of pilgrims and tourists. In this place Fr Couturier was decisive for gaining stained glass windows by Rouault, a crucifix by Germaine Richier, a tapestry by Lurçat, paintings by Matisse and Pierre Bonnard, sculpture by Lipchitz, ceramic by Chagall, mosaic by Léger and a tabernacle bronze by Braque. At Audincourt he was mainly responsible for Léger designing stained glass. At Ronchamp he liaised with Le Corbusier who created one of the most impressive churches of the century. At Vence, in the wake of a young nun who began the process, he was responsible for Matisse's creation and decoration of the Chapel of the Rosary, important, not only for the artist who, in order to create with integrity had to insist that the commissioned architect be de-commissioned, but for the Church as a whole. The mastery in execution and pure, joyful atmosphere are of a high and sacred order. It is a pertinent comment on a theme that runs through this book that Richier's Assy crucifix, a response, not only to a religious commission to represent the tortured death of Christ, but a commission to depict this image against the background of the appalling revelations of World War Two, became an object of hostility since it contradicted familiar images and religious kitsch. The Integrists, traditional Catholics, conducted an orchestrated campaign against it and eventually the Pope issued a Bull ordering its removal. Only with time did it regain its honoured position, eloquent of the suffering of God.

These French developments not only set our story in a wider context, they acted as supports and catalysts for some of the excellent work in England. Spence and Gibberd, for example, were inspired by Couturier, not least by his willingness to employ the best artists and to judge the appropriateness of sacred art by the work itself and not by the individual belief of the artist.

2. The Contemporary Scene

BY DINT OF history the procedures governing the introduction of new art into the Episcopalian churches in the USA are much simpler than they are in England today. So far as cathedrals are concerned any proposal is submitted to the Fabric Committee and, if it is a radical or substantial proposal it may well be submitted to the board of trustees as well. In fact and by convention, however, the Dean sits on these committees and his particular responsibilities cover church decoration. Cases involving sharp disagreement are submitted to the Bishop.

As indicated in the last chapter the case in England is quite different. We have a large heritage and churches date from the Saxon period. A multitude of interests relate to these precious buildings and interests are magnified with the old cathedrals. Archeology, architecture, history, art, liturgy and mission are all included and these interests are far from identical. To prevent the fossilising of churches as museums when still used by the Church the ecclesiastical exemption was successfully negotiated. But since the legitimising agencies were developed in response to the problems outlined in the last chapter historicism and bureaucracy have become part of the system.

Let us consider briefly the structure governing the care of churches and cathedrals in the Church of England. In the case of a parish church any minor proposal must be submitted for the approval of the Parochial Church Council of which the parish priest is the Chairperson. It is then submitted to the Archdeacon, part of whose responsibility to the Bishop is the oversight of the fabric of churches within his jurisdiction. If the proposal seems appropriate the Archdeacon will issue a certificate and the work can proceed. In the case of more substantial proposals the PCC makes a submission to the Diocesan Advisory Committee (DAC). If so minded the DAC will recommend to the

Chancellor of the diocese that the proposal is accepted. If the DAC finds problems with the proposal it may refer back to the PCC or submit it to the Chancellor without commendation. The Chancellor, who is a distinguished lawyer and appointed by the Bishop, makes his own decision, but the views of the DAC are clearly very important.

Diocesan Advisory Committees

The DAC consists of a chairperson, the archdeacons of the diocese, and not less than 12 other persons. The Bishop appoints the Chairperson after consultation with his Council, the Chancellor of the diocese and the Council for the Care of Churches. Not less than ten members are appointed by the Bishop's council, two from the Diocesan Synod, one after consultation with the Historic Buildings and Monuments Commission for England, one after consultation with the relevant associations of local authorities, and one after consultation with the national amenity societies. Other persons may be co-opted.

In making these appointments the Bishop's Council must ensure that the persons appointed have between them: knowledge of the history, development and use of church buildings, knowledge of the liturgy and worship of the Church of England, knowledge of architecture, archaeology, art and history, and experience of the care of historic buildings and their contents.

This structure is the most recent revision of a system that goes back to the thirteenth century. By 1988 discussions between the government and the Churches respecting the continuance of the ecclesiastical exemption clause found agreement in that, so far as the Church of England was concerned, an undertaking was given that 'in future, DACs would have in their membership people who could genuinely be said to represent the interests of the national amenity societies, English Heritage and local planning authorities.' This undertaking represented the good practice that bishops had long observed in making appointments to DACs. 'The Chairman of Coventry DAC, for example, is a member of the Executive Committee of the Georgian Group, the former Chairman of the Chelmsford DAC is now head of the Historic Building's Division, English Heritage and several officers of the London Division of English Heritage sit on the DACs of the two London dioceses, after consultation with the Chief Executive of the County Council, the Deputy Planning Officer (who is also an architect) was appointed to the DAC and has become one of its most useful members'.[1]

The statutory amenity societies mentioned earlier are the Society for the Protection of Ancient Buildings, the Georgian Group, the Victorian Society, the Ancient Monuments Society, the Society and Council for British Archaeology. The Thirties Society has applied for statutory recognition. The underlying philosophy of these societies, which naturally affects Christian thinking about church building, is suggested by the words in the National Heritage Act, 1983, concerning the Historical Buildings and Monuments Commission for England. We read: 'It shall be the duty of the Commission (so far as practicable) (a) to secure the preservation of ancient monuments and historic buildings situated in England, (b) to promote the preservation and enhancement of the character and appearance of conservation areas situated in England and (c) to promote the public enjoyment of, and advance their knowledge of, ancient monuments and historic buildings situated in England, and their preservation.' The Commission 'may give advice to any person in relation to ancient monuments, etc., whether or not they have been consulted'. The Commission members are appointed by the Secretary of State and number not less that eight and not more than seventeen. Those appointed must have knowledge of history, archaeology, architecture, preservation or conservation of monuments or buildings, town and country planning, tourism, commerce and finance. One should have knowledge of local government.

One other important factor should be mentioned. The Church of England Inspection of Churches Measure (1955) made it mandatory for every church in a diocese to have an

1. Report to CCC by the Secretary, Peter Burman, February, 1988

architect approved by the DAC, who makes a quinquennial inspection of the church. His Report suggests the programme of repair for the ensuing five years. An art expert of a particular kind is thus available to the local church community.

In the case of Winchester diocese the DAC is comprised by the Chairman, who is a retired general and distinguished engineer, a priest who is a church historian, two lay women who are prepared to serve the Committee, four architects, a building conservationist, a priest with a music degree, a bell-ringer with knowledge of architecture, an archaeologist, an architectural historian, specialising in stained glass, a priest with an interest in sound systems, the Cathedral Curator, once a museum curator, invited to join the Committee as a specialist 'for fine art and silver'.[2] The Diocesan Assistant Secretary serves as secretary.

Such a committee is clearly weighted on the conservationist side, but it would be unfair to draw general conclusions too rapidly. The architects and stained glass specialist might encourage new creation of a high order when appropriate. The judgement must lie in what happens in parish churches rather than what profession is represented on the committee. The experience of the letterer Alec Peever, who has just completed five years on the Oxford DAC and has resigned for personal reasons has been encouraging. Bearing in mind that he is an excellent and practising letterer, for six years he was a member of the Oxford DAC, it being a practice of that DAC to include a practising artist on its committee. In answer to a questionnaire he says that his views as an artist were always taken seriously; that the DAC regarded aesthetic criteria as very important, the problem being to persuade donors to use good practitioners; that parishes occasionally approach the DAC, but that members of the DAC always visit parishes when appropriate; that the DAC keeps a register of approved artists which is 'quite good'; that there would be a value in a diocese appointing a qualified person to assist parishes to find good artists; that the DAC does not promote art in the diocese except through

2. DAC Minutes, 8 Jan. 86

its necessary work; parishes can consult the CCC register of artists, the Regional Arts Board have slide indices, and local parishes can compile their own dossier of approved artists.[1]

I was generously permitted to examine in detail the minutes of the Winchester DAC, 1983–93. The Committee clearly had a full agenda and worked strenuously. Site visits were often made and difficult cases were generally dealt with expertly and tolerantly, so long as the expertise related to conservation and routine matters, and the assessing rather than the initiating role of the Committee is borne in mind. It was difficult to categorise the multitude of cases coming before the Committee; some could be variously assessed, others covered more than one category, some passed through different stages before completion. My approximate analysis reveals for the period 1983–93:

Category of Case	*Number*
Predominant aesthetic component	548
Predominant building improvement component	507
Predominant repair component	502
Conservation	36
Sale of valuables	20
	Total 1613

Council for the Care of Churches

It was mentioned earlier that the CCC, having begun in embryo in 1917 at the Victoria and Albert Museum, was founded formally in 1921 as the centre of a network of DACs. It is a permanent commission of the General Synod of the Church of England. Its functions are to assist the Synod in matters relating to the use, care and planning or designing of places on worship; to maintain contact with other official bodies of the Church of England and other churches, Government departments and other recognised bodies, so far as they are concerned with the Council's work; to allocate funds for the care and embellishment of churches and advise

1. From questionnaire supplied by the author, 1994

grant-making agencies seeking its help; to conduct discussions on behalf of the Church of England with professional bodies connected with the inspection and repair of churches; to develop and maintain the survey of English churches and a library of books, technical information, photographic and other material to enable the efficient despatch of the Council's work; to carry out educational work to raise standards of appreciation and to promote research and publicise methods of conservation and redevelopment of churches; 'to promote the encouragement of artistic creativity' and to foster the development of a ministry to tourists; to advise and help DACs and other concerned diocesan officials and committees; to work closely with the Cathedral Fabric Commission for England (CFCE) in matters of mutual concern.

The Council consists of a Chairperson and up to 22 other members, at least six of whom are members of the General Synod. The Standing Committee of the General Synod is responsible for the appointment of members, though consultation with various bodies is mandatory. The standing Committee must provide members with expertise in archaeology, architecture, archives, art, history and liturgy.

At the time of writing the Chairman is the Bishop of Hulme. In addition there are seven clergymen, a specialist in metal work (Claude Blair), a stained glass specialist (Peter Cormack) and four others with a general interest in the work of the Council.

It is difficult to assess the value of the work given by these authorising bodies to local churches. We may begin with some words of Judith Scott, whose practical knowledge as Secretary of the CCC must be unique. At a Conference on Church Building in London 1945–58, held on 21 January, 1988, she said that during the Second World War 624 of the 701 Anglican churches in London were damaged, and 91 totally destroyed. Severe losses were sustained in other major English cities. There followed a programme of repair and new building. Reflection on that programme is worthwhile in giving the background to much contemporary concern and practice. In 1961 the CCC commented in its 15th

Report that the last fifteen years had witnessed a church
building programme comparable to that in the latter half of
the nineteenth century. 'Unfortunately, however, the quality
of the buildings themselves is not always worthy of the
efforts made to provide them, compared with the many
interesting and distinguished new churches being erected on
the continent, especially in France and Germany. Ours, in
many cases, seem to lack vitality and fitness for purpose.'
Miss Scott's Report comes then to the crux, 'For this sad state
of affairs the Council is often unjustly blamed. Under the
present system neither they nor the DACs are required to be
consulted about the design of new churches: in the case of
parish churches the Church Commissioners are required to
pronounce that the structure is sound, and the Archdeacon
that the ornaments are legal and THAT IS ALL.' She
concluded, 'I do not think the Church is to be commended,
in London or elsewhere, for its post-war building record, but
I do think the attendant circumstances to deserve more
careful study'.[1]

At the same meeting, Peter Burman, who had succeeded
Judith Scott as Secretary of the CCC commended a paper by
Neil Burton (a previous CCC Pastoral Measure Officer) to
CCC members. Burton alleged that few pamphlets had been
produced giving guidelines on church buildings. By contrast,
on the continent there had been much debate including
architects, liturgists and others. The mainspring had been
the Liturgical movement and the recognition that the administration of the sacraments needs an appropriate architectural
setting. A crucial German document, a product of the
German Liturgical Commission, published in 1947 and translated in 1949, had been passed over almost without
comment.[2]

Such malaise, even though hard to quantify, should be set
in a broader cultural context. It is difficult to think of the
architectural additions in the city of London since the war
with pride or even equanimity. Although the Georgian city of

1. CCC archives
2. CCC archives

Chichester was declared eventually an area of special conservation the depradations due to the local authority called forth an amenity society of 3,000 strong in protest at the mediocrity that passed for enhancement. Thinking of the artistic world as a whole Malcolm Yorke declared that those governing taste and governing in war and post-war years were 'essentially conservative and timid'.[1]

By the year 1977 Peter Burman, now secretary of the CCC, could say, 'No one who visits churches as a regular part of his existence can doubt that the overwhelming majority are remarkably well cared for and loved. Those who have been visiting them for much longer lives than mine add also that churches are cared for today as never before'.[2] This testimony, from one who knew the truth better than most must be given its full weight. It cannot be doubted that the affection and commitment of local priests, PCCs and congregations were responsible mainly for this improvement and the adjudicating authority of the bodies we have discussed channelled and heightened the quality of local effort.

Here are two extracts, taken almost at random, from the minutes of Winchester DAC, illustrative of its best work. The Committee discussed a plea for advice from Bentley PCC regarding a new altar frontal. 'In response to a request for advice it was suggested that the parish approach, Belinda, Lady Montagu, an expert in all matters of embroidery.'[3] On 13 April 1983 the DAC considered an application from St Peter's PCC, Beech, for a memorial. We read, 'The PCC was encouraged to find a suitable craftsman to make the memorial'. At the meeting held on 11 May 1983 we find that the names of Simon Verity and David Kindersley are given.

Let us consider in more detail two difficult cases. The first concerns the Church of All Saints', Basingstoke. I was team vicar in the parish of Basingstoke from 1981 to 1987, with special responsibility for All Saints' Church. In January 1983, the various authorising committees permitted the introduc-

---

1. *The Spirit of Place*, p. 159, Constable, 1988
2. M. Binney and P. Burman, *Change and Decay*, p. 171, Studio Vista, 1977
3. 13 July 83

tion of Elisabeth Frink's *Head of Christ* in the Bapistry of All Saints', a fine Temple Moore building consecrated in 1917. In 1985 application was made for stained glass to be introduced into the two side windows at the west end, each one having two lights, from a design by Cecil Collins and the glass to be made by Patrick Reyntiens. An angel, with echoes of Byzantine inspiration, was proposed for each light and the colouring was in whites, yellows, golds, with some brown lines. At their first meeting the Committee minuted that 'while wishing to encourage parishes to commission works of artists of this calibre it was felt that the proposed site was not really suitable. The two windows at the west end ... were never meant to have attention drawn to them; and because of internal partitions the visibility is interrupted preventing a clear view of the figures. If the church is to become a centre of excellence (*vide* Frink sculpture case 5540 January 1983), the DAC would prefer consideration given to the great west window as a site for some stained glass work.'[1] The difficulties were reported to Collins and Reyntiens who promised to take the visibility aspect into consideration. The DAC later minuted that, while not withdrawing its earlier comments it 'would not oppose the scheme prepared by Collins and Reyntiens'.[2]

The enterprise and supervision thus far can be seen to be excellent. The DAC had legitimate hesitations but recognised that the area of consideration could be variously assessed and that, in the persons of Collins and Reyntiens, two prominent English artists took a different view from that of the Committee. They gave credit to the living artists working the actual site and in the event their humility was justified. What the Committee could not know was that an impecunious church had the greatest difficulty raising the money even for these smaller windows and had in mind one day to tackle the problem of the great west window.

In 1987 the DAC made a minute referring to a design by Collins, to be made into stained glass by Reyntiens, for the

1. Winchester DAC minutes, 10 April 1995
2. Winchester DAC minutes, 10 April 1985

great west window. More than £46,000 had been raised by two people without drawing on ordinary church funds and the design had been agreed by the Church Committee, the PCC and came now before the DAC. The design showed God through the image of the sun, with wheeling circles of winged angels surrounding the central image. The minute reads, 'The drawing of the proposed window ... was not recommended. The drawing did not give a clear impression of the finished work, being inaccurate in some architectural detail and showing no lead lines nor saddle bars. Even allowing for that, the committee was not happy with the overall effect of the blaze of yellow and, indeed, thought that the initial impression given by the design was that of a sun god rather than a Christian image. The intended meaning of the design would come through only from reading a written interpretation of it.'[1]

Had I, as patron of the proposed work of art, and chairman of the Church Committee in whose church the window would be placed accepted this ruling, as it was intended that I should, a great work of art would have been lost to the Church and humanity in an age when such works are rare. A project so important, with such artists and money involved, should have included dialogue outside the constraints of committee. Bureaucracy was smothering creativity. Second, if the reader consults the qualifications required for CCC and DAC members he will find no reference to theology. There is reference to liturgy and worship, which is an aspect of theology, but it is not stressed and may be of a historicist or practical nature. Questions of valid images are central to the problem of Christian communication in our time. It so happens that I was convinced that the Committee was quite wrong in its disparaging remark about pagan imagery. In the Christian tradition God had been imaged as the sun in Old and New Testaments and throughout the period of the Church. Reference to the need of written interpretation simply emphasises the narrowness a verbal and literary culture inculcates in people. The simple

1. Winchester DAC minutes 8 July 1987

and archetypal image of the sun with angels would be hampered by words and words can at best only suggest the truth it communicates. That the image is symbolic rather than anecdotal is perfectly valid, and it may be argued that in a culture that has lost its biblical base it is preferable. Complaint about the absence of saddle bars and lead lines overlooks the fact that in dealing with one of England's leading stained glass artists, and one who is long and widely experienced, trust should have been given. A scrutinising committee easily forgets that a design is only the general reality of what will be created. The artist wished to be left free to integrate the lead lines and saddle bars into his design as he actually created. We are touching here the possible defects of any committee procedure, which tends to be legalistic.

One further point of singular importance must be made. At the outset of this whole project Cecil Collins sat in All Saints' Church and discovered that some fructiying experience was at work within in him. He told me, 'I will only reveal what has always been there.' In the area of the baptistry, with font surmounted by Frink's bronze Head of Christ, Collins found his iconographical root in the story of the baptism of Jesus. Circles became important because of the overwhelming masculinity of vertical lines in the window frame. The sun emerged partly because the atmosphere in the church was one of spiritual joy. Thus knowledge of Scripture, actual location, present atmosphere and penetration of Being brought to birth through the artist that over which he had no conscious control. The window design was his prayer. Committees with long agendas are not well placed to judge such matters.

I decided to risk my job by challenging the Committee. The details do not matter now but I was kindly invited to join the Committee and I sent in advance a letter of explanation by Patrick Reyntiens and a commendation by the Rev Professor John Bowker. The DAC minute reads, 'The Revd Dr K. Walker spoke in answer to the letter which had been sent to him following the previous meeting. He also read letters from Mr Patrick Reyntiens and the Revd Professor

John Bowker ... which responded to the committee's comment on the technical and theological aspects of the proposed design. Dr Walker drew the committee's attention to the interest taken in All Saints' by the CCC and, in particular, the article in *Churchscape, 1986,* referring to and illustrating the two earlier windows by Cecil Collins. After answering members' questions Dr Walker left the meeting.

After discussion it was agreed that the committee recognised the high competence of both the artist and the glass maker and would have to trust them. The committee was unable to advise the Chancellor further.' Voting: 6 in favour; 0 against; 4 abstentions.

On this occasion the DAC showed magnanimity in face of credible opposition to their previous view. The Chancellor speedily granted a faculty.

So far as I was concerned personally, the whole enterprise could have foundered without the assistance of a wise team rector, who insisted that individual churches within the team ministry should be followed by the rest on this kind of project. Wise clergy and laity are not always abundant and the questioning of the project by the final authorising committee could well have been fatal. Layers of bureaucracy where high contemporary art is concerned may not be helpful. Secondly, whilst modesty is rightly enjoined upon us praise is recognised as an important incentive in work. I am not aware of looking for or specially wanting praise, but I recall that it was persons outside the Church who have congratulated me on notable commissions. Why should not the DAC and Bishop publicise good practice within their diocese, partly to extend its range?

The second instructive example is that of the memorial window proposed for St Peter and St Paul Church, King's Somborne. Sir Thomas Sopwith lived in the village for forty years, dying at the age of 101. From humble beginning his enterprising spirit and engineering brilliance made him an aircraft designer, including military aircraft such as the Sopwith Pup and the Sopwith Camel, used in World War One, the Hawker Hurricane used in World War Two, and more recently, the Harrier Jump Jet. He loved sailing and was involved in the production of the Endeavour yacht, which competed in the America's Cup race.

After much discussion the PCC decided to erect a memorial to Sopwith in the local church and the idea of a stained glass window at the west end found favour. A working party was set up that reported regularly to the PCC and a design was eventually approved. It showed the local church together with the aircraft and yacht associated with Sopwith and a scroll at the bottom gave the commemoration. This was submitted to the DAC in 1989 and rejected on grounds of style. The DAC stained glass advisor came to the parish to offer advice and another design was submitted to the DAC in 1990, drawn up by a member of the working party. This design incorporated the three generations with which Sopwith had been involved, his love of sailing and the Endeavour yacht, and a commemorative scroll with Sopwith's coat of arms. A fund was launched to raise £6,000 required for the work, and a local firm of glassmakers was engaged.

In the meantime a new vicar had arrived. He used the parish magazine to raise serious objections to the design. The vicar stated that the design was 'devoid of any religious content and from that point of view not within the historical tradition of stained glass windows in our churches'. He quoted Herbert's famous lines, 'A man that looks on glass ...' and asked if the window should take such a prominent place in the church and whether it fulfilled the deeper reality so vividly expressed in Herbert's lines.[1] The design became public debate and when, in 1992, the PCC considered the objections lodged to the Faculty application they felt they had no alternative but to begin again.

A new design was commissioned for the PCC to consider. It featured the village Lutyens war memorial, a crusader's cross taken from the decoration of the church, the River Test, two aircraft and the yacht Endeavour, together with an inscription bearing Sopwith's name. The design was displayed in church and some objections were made. It was

1. October, 1991

submitted to the DAC, who felt it was not satisfactory. Modifications were made and the revised design was re-submitted. In 1993 the Chancellor considered the application for a faculty and sought first the views of English Heritage, the local planning authority, as it was an old church, and the CCC. English Heritage and the CCC were against the proposal believing the design 'lacks artistic unity and boldness of vision'. The Chancellor cautioned the PCC against pressing the application, which would mean a consistory court hearing that could prove expensive. The PCC accepted the Chancellor's decision and, at the time of writing, are considering asking the advice of the CCC about a competent artist.

No doubt any substantial enterprise can founder, all the more so when so many voices must be heeded, but it does seem that much unnecessary trouble has been created in this case. If the advice of Bishop Bell, quoted in the last chapter had been acted upon, a diocesan or regional officer would have been available to advise the parish. Since the DAC and CCC are authorising bodies they are not well placed to provide this, and their culture is of a more conserving than innovative nature. Christian conviction is unlikely to enthuse English Heritage or the local authority and they are again ingrained in a culture unlikely to choose well in a project of this nature.

It is also noteworthy that no one seems to have raised the liturgical appropriateness of any of the designs for this prominent position in the church. The medievals would have been most unlikely to have made this error, and it empha-sises the importance of theological qualification being repre-sented on the DAC and CCC. Given an understanding of the right symbolism for such a window in such a position, to be made by the best artist available, a quite exceptional achievement might have resulted. Granted the reputation of Sopwith money would have been forthcoming for a project seen to be exceptional.[1]

---

1. *Hampshire Chronicle*, 6.3.1992. After writing this account the Hampshire Chronicle, 9.2.1996 reported that John Hayward's design of Archangel Michael casting out the devil has been authorised. The news is good.

In passing, mention must be made of redundant churches, some of them works of art and some containing works of art. Dioceses are responsible for seeking alternative uses for redundant churches. If nothing is found they pass to the care of the Churches Conservation Trust or the Diocesan Board of Finance, or demolition. The Department of the Environment may conduct a non-statutory public enquiry into the proposed demolition of any listed building or one in a conservation area. £23.9 million has been raised from the disposal of redundant churches and sites. £3 million has passed to the Churches Conservation Trust, financed jointly with the Government on a 30%/70% basis. 54 redundancy schemes were approved in 1993, including 8 which amended earlier schemes. New uses were found for 36 of the buildings and 9 schemes provided for partial or total demolition. In four of these places a new church has been built. Nine churches of high merit were passed to the Churches Conservation Trust. Since the 1969 Pastoral Measure came into operation 1,387 churches have been declared redundant and had their future settled. 771 have found alternative use, 313 had been demolished, and 303 have been preserved.[1]

Complex or controversial cases of faculty application are usually referred by the Chancellor of a diocese to the CCC for comment, as was the case with the Sopwith window mentioned earlier. In 1988 there were 38 cases so referred. In 1992 the number had risen to 69 and in addition 48 cases were considered for redundancy.

The CCC is itself funded by the General Synod, being one of its permanent commissions. In addition, it is the recipient of grants and bequests which it distributes. About £200,000 a year is given to local churches, mainly for the repair of fabric and furnishings. The crisis in funding for conservation work was graphically illustrated in an article which appeared in *Country Life* and written by Richard Haslam.[2] The author estimated that 75% of the wall-paintings made in England between 1100 and 1500 had been lost. The loss of wood

---

1. *Church Commissioners Report and Accounts*, 1993
2. 1 Dec. 1988

sculpture had been even more severe. There remains about 2,000 medieval wall-paintings or schemes in England. For conservation £250,000 is available annually from English Heritage and the National Heritage Memorial Fund. The CCC had £14,000 from all sources for conservation of all paintings in 1987. Parish Churches raised £52,000. English Heritage offered £25,000. Unfortunately £189,000 was needed and 51% of what was required was not met. Proceeds from the National Lottery have relieved already this crisis but it is too early to judge the long-term effect.

The CCC has as part of its brief an educational function to raise standards of appreciation and to promote appreciation and the encouragement of artistic creativity. To this end it organises conferences where serious issues are discussed by informed people and art of an instructive kind may be displayed, or sites visited where good sacred art and architecture may be seen. Almost yearly in recent times a conference for artists and craftspersons has been held at its own headquarters. Clergy, potential clients and members of DACs have joined these day events. I wish to pay credit for the notable addresses I have heard and the facility provided by the conference setting to meet persons important for my interest in sacred visual art. In 1986 the conference addressed the subject of Icons. The Revd John Baggley, who had published recently a book on the subject spoke about the place of icons in the tradition of theology and spirituality. Richard Temple, an icon gallery owner and acknowledged authority on icons spoke about the history and tradition of icons. Canon Allchin spoke about the use of icons in prayer and spirituality. Worship and discussion were as usual part of the day.

In 1987 Churches and Tourism, Monuments' Conservation in Churches and The Creative Artist and the Church were the subjects addressed. The speakers at this last conference were Edith Reyntiens, the icon painter, Leonard Rosoman, the painter and wall-painter, who was engaged in painting Lambeth Palace Chapel ceiling, and Dr Alan Powers, the art historian. 95 people attended. In 1988 Church Lighting, Through a Glass darkly, or Lightly ... (stained glass!), and

Towards a Higher Standard of Church Textiles? were the
subjects discussed. At the conference on stained glass
Thomas Denny, Mark Angus, Anthony Holloway and Joseph
Nuttgens spoke about making stained glass in churches and
cathedrals, and David Pearce, Sally Scott, Jennifer Conway
and Alfred Fisher spoke about glass engraving in churches
and cathedrals. At the conference on textiles Beryl Deane
gave the keynote lecture, Michael Reardon, cathedral and
church architect spoke about textiles from his professional
standpoint and David Gazeley of Watts and Co., Peter
Collingwood, a weaver, and Jane Lemon, much concerned in
reviving textiles in churches and cathedral in Salisbury
diocese, spoke about their work. 106 people attended.

Reporting on the 1989 conference Letter Cutting and
Sculpture Peter Burman quoted one of the speakers, Susan
Morrison, as saying that she relished visiting the diploma
shows of London colleges of art and contrasted the 'energy,
commitment and dynamism' which the young sculptors
bring to their work with current church art where these
factors are often lacking. He quoted also a letter to him by
the Archdeacon of Nottingham, who agreed with the principle of encouraging individual letter cutters working memorials, but who added that it would be a long time before such
practice became habitual.

Annual CCC conferences take place in a particular
diocese, varying each year, for DAC members throughout the
Church of England. The conferences for the last five years
have been: 1990, Chelmsford, Space and Light; 1991,
Sheffield, Citizens of No Mean City: the Problems and
Potential of the Urban Church; 1992, Bury St Edmunds, The
Churches and the Crafts, Then and Now; 1993 Exeter,
Church Tourism and the Environment; 1994, Worcester, How
we Work a DAC. At the 1992 Conference the Minister of
Agriculture considered changes in Suffolk. Dr John Blatchly
spoke about Enjoying Suffolk Churches and there was a tour
of significant Suffolk Churches. The architect S. Dykes
Bowers spoke about Church Architecture in the Twentieth
Century. Dr Veronica Sekules followed with 'The Use of
Church Furnishings in the Middle Ages'. An architect and a

parish priest addressed the subject of the use of churches today. There was a visit to the cathedral and Abbey ruins. The Registrar of the diocese and others led a discussion on living with the new measures governing the maintenance and embellishment of churches, and there was a live exhibition and workshops on the subjects of the Conference.

From time to time the CCC organises training days for archdeacons, DAC chairmen and secretaries.

The CCC produces a number of cheap but informed booklets for use by those concerned with care of churches. How to Look after your Church (1989) gives guidelines for spotting fabric trouble and whom to inform in case of difficulty. In addition the CCC maintains a library of about 12,000 books on the history, art, architecture of churches and other pertinent matter, records of completed conservation projects, a slide and photograph library of artists and craftpersons.

This whole educational and resource facility of the CCC is vital for the Church, helping to stimulate interest and discrimination, where these may not be immediately apparent. Most of the lectures I have attended have been accompanied by slides and the best of these were inspiring and deeply educational. The testimony of a person like Beryl Deane was wonderful to hear. The criticism must be, however, that the conferences have not always been as demanding or as radical (meaning to go to the roots) as they should be. There is so much prejudice to overcome, so much vision to be imparted, that one wonders if conferences might not be fewer and the association with, say, the Arts Council, fostered so that the best in contemporary textiles or some such medium might not be on view and spoken about by those who understand them best. Having used the slide library the criticism might be along the same lines. Should not the CCC bravely judge quality in admitting slide representation of artists' work and, by knowing to whom to refer enquirers enable discrimination to increase in the recommendation of particular artists for particular commissions? That misunderstanding about the importance of the Council's work is widespread is clear from an informal poll referred to by Dr Thomas Cocke, Secretary of CCC, in 1991, which revealed that half the parishes in the Church of England had never heard of it.

Dr Cocke prepared for the Council an interesting paper, *The CCC Strategy for 2000*. There is listed as matters of concern: Resources, Administration, Books, Conservation and finally to promote high standards in architecture and furnishing for new churches 'to the promotion of contemporary art in general and to the maintenance of its Register of Artists and Craftsmen in particular. However, it can be seen as a diversion from the primary concern of the Council with the care and conservation of what already exists'. In a later version[1], this paragraph became 'to the promotion of contemporary art in general and the maintenance of the Register of Artists and Craftsmen in particular, and so it is logical that it promotes high standards both in the architecture and in the furnishings of new churches. As the Decade of Evangelism advances, such guidance is increasingly important.' There is revealed here the possibly unresolved tension in the Council between the demands of conservation and the opportunities of new creation.

Legislation Governing Cathedrals

Until recently control of cathedrals has lain effectively with Deans, Provosts and Chapters. Judith Scott was in a good position to judge how the transition was made to the present position and her brief anecdotal tale, recorded earlier, is worth recalling (pp. 42–43 above).

Some time prior to the introduction of the new legislation governing cathedrals Peter Burman, reporting on the role and function of the CCC had written, 'Associated with the Council is the Cathedrals Advisory Committee for England, whose comprehensive remit is to give help and advice in plans and problems affecting the fabric, furnishings, fittings and precincts of cathedrals. Although English cathedrals are autonomous, they usually welcome advice on the many developments which they propose, especially since they are

---

1. 19 Oct. 1992

almost inevitably subject to intense public scrutiny.' Three factors in particular combined to change this charmed position. First, it is part of democratic understanding that every person or party with responsibility should be accountable. The privilege of Deans and Chapters seemed anomolous in church and state. Second, the decisions of some chapters respecting their fabric and furnishings seemed to qualified persons sometimes bizarre and mistaken. We shall consider later the case of the conservation of the West Front of Wells Cathedral. The controversy was national headline news and brought Henry Moore and others into the fray. Introducing the new legislation, Bishop Eric Kempe was thought to have justice on his side when he asked if four of five clergymen should decide the future of the West Front of Wells Cathedral?[1] Third, it was recognized that cathedrals needed vast sums of money to maintain their fabric, but substantial state aid would only be forthcoming if the supervision of the fabric of cathedrals was equivalent, and related, to the state system. In 1989 the General Synod, despite some dissentient voices from deans and provosts, approved the Care of Cathedrals Measure.

The first statement of the measure is that the care and conservation of a cathedral must 'have due regard to the fact that the cathedral church is a seat of the bishop and a centre of worship and mission'. It goes on to say that 'the administrative body of a cathedral must not implement any proposal' which would materially affect 'the architectural, archaeological, artistic or historic character' of the cathedral, its precincts and setting; nor shall any object be sold, loaned or disposed of which has 'architectural, archaeological, artistic or historic interest', or make permanent addition of any object which would 'materially affect the architectural,

---

1. Salisbury Cathedral may have been one catalyst for change of control. Roy Spring relates that during the late 1950s and early 1960s much of Scott's interior conservation work was undone, 'Skidmore's screen was sold for scrap along with the communion rails. The Minton tiles were removed, and buried in the grounds of the Palace. The reredos was broken up and dispersed. In the Chapter House two windows were removed and the 1860 glass destroyed. As a result of this Wyattism complaints and criticisms mounted, resulting in the formation of the Cathedrals Advisory Commission'. Cf. *Salisbury Cathedral*, p. 29, Unwin Hyman, 1987

archaeological, artistic, or historic character of the cathedral church' without the approval of the Fabric Advisory Committee (FAC) and possibly the Cathedrals Fabric Commission for England (CFCE).

The duty of the CFCE is to advise the administrative body of a cathedral and the FAC on the care, conservation, repair or development of the cathedral; to determine any application made to it by the administrative body of a cathedral; to promote cooperation between the Commission and organisations concerned with the care and study of buildings of architectural, archeaological, artistic or historic interest in England; to assist the administrative bodies of cathedrals by participating in educational and research projects which will promote the care, conservation, repair or development of cathedrals; to maintain jointly with the CCC a library of books, photographs etc. of material relating to cathedrals.

It is the duty of the FAC to advise the administrative body of a cathedral on the care, conservation, repair or development of the cathedral; to consider and determine an application made to it by the administrative body. The CFCE may call in any application made to the FAC if it would permanently alter the cathedral. Applications for approval of proposals to FACs must be displayed publicly, sent to the CFCE and sometimes to the local planning authority. Applications to the CFCE are notified to the FAC, the Historic Buildings and Monuments Commission and the national amenity societies. Before determining an application the CFCE will consider any representations made to it. The administrative body of a cathedral may appeal against the decision of the FAC to the CFCE. Appeals beyond this end with the Commission of Review, whose decision is final.

The CFCE consists of 24 persons. The Chairperson is appointed by the Archbishops of Canterbury and York after consultation with the Secretary of State for the Environment. The archbishops appoint the other members after consulting various bodies. One member 'shall be a painter, sculptor, or other artist, with experience of work for a cathedral or other churches', and the President of the Royal Academy of Art must first be consulted. Seven members are appointed who between them have 'special knowledge of archaeology, architecture, archives, art, the care of books and manuscripts, history (including the history of art and architecture), and liturgy (including church music)'.

The FAC consists of between three and five members appointed by the administrative body after consultation with the CFCE, who are not in Holy Orders or employed by the administrative body, between three and five members appointed by the CFCE after consultation with the administrative body, being persons with special knowledge of the care and maintenance of buildings of outstanding architectural or historic interest and a particular interest in the cathedral church concerned. The Committee appoints its chairperson from its members. The dean or provost and residentiary canons may attend meetings and speak, but not vote. The cathedral architect and archaeological consultant must attend meetings.

In 1987 the CAC consisted of 20 members and in addition Peter Burman, Secretary of the CAC, Jeffrey West, Cathedrals' Assistant (CAC), and Dr Richard Gem (Departmental Secretary, CAC). The chairperson was Professor Peter Lasko, of the Courtauld Institute, and among its members were five clergymen, the architect of Durham Cathedral, the sometime architect of York, Norwich and St Paul's Cathedrals, and sometime Director of ICCROM, the Curator in Administration at the Victoria and Albert Museum, knowledgeable in twentieth century art, an art historian, sometime, Professor at the Courtauld Institute, the Duke of Grafton, Chairman of the Society for the Protection of Ancient Buildings, a Commissioner of English Heritage, an engineer, a cathedral librarian, a sculptor (Mr Michael Kenny) a Royal Fine Art Commissioner having close links with the National Trust, a cathedral archaeologist at Bristol, Lichfield and Wells Cathedrals. At the time of writing the CFCE consists of 17 members. The Chairperson was previously Headmaster of Eton College, and currently Master of Corpus Christi College, Cambridge, a retired professor of the Courtauld Institute, the keeper of ceramics at the Victoria and Albert Museum and authority on stained glass, a conservation architect, two cathedral architects and a retired cathedral architect, who was previously Director of ICCROM, two engineers, Mr Geoffrey Clarke, R.A. sculptor and painter, a commissioner of English Heritage, a Royal Fine Art Commissioner having close links with the National Trust, a Cathedral Archaeologist at Bristol, Lichfield and Wells Cathedrals, two liturgists, an authority on organs, and the Curator in Administration at the Victoria and Albert Museum, knowledgeable on twentieth century art.

Such committees command respect considering the scope of their specialist knowledge and the distinction of some of their members. Decisions on artistic matters would depend on how openly the actual artists are listened to in committees weighted on the side of conservation. In a private letter to the author Mr Geoffrey Clarke writes: 'I should encourage an architect member of the R.A. to take my place. Practically all that appears on the agenda is concerned with archaeology, preservation, or the thoroughly academic. The selection and encouragement of art is largely down to each cathedral.'[1]

The membership of FACs varies with each cathedral. I have two complete lists to hand. In the first the Chairperson is a professor of History and Archaeology. The other members include a historian, a sculptor (K. Carter), a retired architect, a professor of English, a textiles worker, an archaeologist, and a surveyor. A retired school master is Chairperson in the second list. The other members include a retired military engineer, two archaeologists, two architects, a painter (Thetis Blacker), a medieval historian, and a medieval paintings' conservationist from the Courtauld Institute. So far as I have been able to discover visual art is represented on FACs as follows: Chichester, Richard Marks, Curator, Brighton Pavillion and Curator of the Dean Hussey Collection; Bury St Edmunds, Peter Cormack, Curator, William Morris Museum, Walthamstow; Exeter, K. Carter, sculptor; Lincoln, Peter Eugune Ball, sculptor and Pamela, Lady Wedgwood, art historian; Southwell, Peter Eugune Balls, sculptor; Winchester, Thetis Blacker, painter;

---

1. Author's archive, 3 Aug. 1994

Rochester, Dr J. Physick, sculpture historian, Roger de Grey, R.A., painter; Newcastle, Fenwick Lawson, sculptor; Truro, Patrick Heron; Manchester, Alaister Smith, Director, Whitworth Art Gallery; Chelmsforth, the Revd Peter Parker, art historian, Richard Stokes, Director, Minories Art gallery; Norwich, Professor Andrew Martindale, art historian, Veronica Sekules, Sainsbury Centre for Visual Arts; Salisbury, Sir John Tooley, committed to the arts and Covent Garden Opera House. Clearly the effort has been made to include artists and art historians in FACs. The effectiveness of the committee will, once more, depend on how openly members listen to the artist when the corporate membership is weighed in a conservationist direction.

So far as the CAC was involved in the decisions of Deans or Provosts and Chapters respecting new works of art we find in 1988 that Hereford introduced a new nave altar platform and Vicar's Choral Cloister; Chichester introduced a bronze sculpture of the Virgin and Child by John Skelton (made in 1966); St Albans introduced a rose window in the north transept by Alan Younger; Durham introduced a new altar frontal in the nine altars' chapel to a design by the Revd Leonard Childs; a reredos was also approved. Guildford introduced a stained glass window by Mark Angus. Certainly other work in different idioms was commissioned and introduced and we are confirmed in believing that whatever might be said concerning quality Cathedrals are active in introducing new and needed artistic work.

The following table indicates the busy agenda the CAC managed:

year	meetings	items	Cathedrals	projects	site visits
1986	9	211	25	44	10
1987	10	212	31	46	10
1988	10	209	29	49	8
1989	10	199	31		5
1990	10	194	21	49	9

In 1992 the CFCE held 10 meetings, conducted 216 items of business and the FACs were operating in 41 cathedrals. In 29 cathedrals applications had been made to the FACS and there were 134 such applications. In 1993 the CFCE met 10 times and conducted 216 items of business. 39 Applications had been received from 20 cathedrals. 97 Applications had been made to FACs from 21 cathedrals.

That the new system of control over cathedrals is believed to be working well is clear from the fact that for the year 1995–6 English Heritage is making a grant of £4,339,000 to thirty cathedrals, for urgent repairs, conservation and fire prevention. This represents an increase of £150,000 on the previous year's award. Ely Cathedral is the largest beneficiary receiving £650,000. All that has been outlined in this chapter would suggest that care and maintenance in Church of England churches and cathedrals are now of a professional standard, and bear comparison with the grants given to churches, consequent upon the professional supervision they have received for a much longer period. Between 1977–1988 £14 million was given to 3,000 churches and chapels.[1]

In the short period during which the CFCF/FAC system has operated no proper analysis can be made in respect of the embellishment of cathedrals. Additions have certainly been made. In 1991 we find two stained glass windows inserted at Gloucester Cathedral, made by Caroline Swash and Thomas Denny; at Worcester the process began to add a wrought iron gate in St John's Chapel; at Hereford a splendid corona was designed and made by Simon Beer to hang above the altar; in 1992 a stained glass window, designed by Leonard Evetts was added to the Galilee Chapel in Durham Cathedral; at Lichfield new candle holders were added in the west gallery; at Winchester a major textiles' programme was proposed; at St Albans a shrine canopy was accepted; at Bradford a new altar with wooden cross and a new hanging embellishing St Aidan's Chapel; in 1993 a sculpture by Antony Gormley for the crypt of Winchester Cathedral; at York an appliqué embroidered panel was replaced by a mosaic panel designed by Graeme Wilson; at Carlisle an

---

1. *SPAB News*, vol 9, no 3, Summer, 1988

'Flight into Egypt' by Margaret Neve, 1987.
Oil on wood panel, 25.4 x 29.2 cm (10 x 11$^{1}/_{2}$ in)

'Mary and the Archangel' by Margaret Neve, 1994.
Oil on wood panel, 58.4 x 63.5 cm (23 x 25 in)

'Jesus is stripped of his Garments' by Albert Herbert, 1987. Oil on canvas, 35.5 x 27.9 cm (14 x 11 in)

'Eve in the Garden, Jonah in the Whale, Noah in the Ark, and the House of God' by Albert Herbert, 1990. Oil on board, 58.4 x 20.3 cm (23^1/$_2$ x 8 in)

'Jesus is taken down from the Cross' by Albert Herbert, 1987. Oil on canvas, 35.5 x 27.9 cm (14 x 11 in)

'Sound II' (Winchester Cathedral) by Antony Gormley,
1986/7. Sculpture in lead, 1.8 metres high (6 feet)

'Madonna and Child'
(St Matthew's Church, Northampton)
by Henry Moore, 1944.

'Lazarus' (Erected 1952 in New College,
Oxford) by Jacob Epstein, carved 1949
Hopton Wood stone.

'Agnus Dei' (Epiphany Chapel, Winchester Cathedral)
by Eric Gill, c.1920. Hopton Wood stone

'Baptistry window' (Coventry Cathedral) designed by
John Piper and made by Patrick Reyntiens, for the
Consecration in 1962.

'Christ before the Judge' (on temporary loan to Winchester Cathedral from the Tate) by Cecil Collins, re-worked 1956. Oil on board, 120.6 x 90 cm (47$^{1}/_{2}$ x 35$^{1}/_{2}$ in) (Photo: Clive Hicks ARPS)

'The Angels' window (All Saints' Church, Basingstoke) designed by Cecil Collins and made by Patrick Reyntiens, unveiled in 1985.

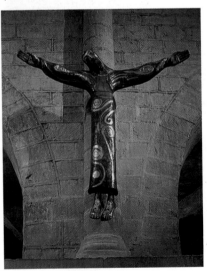

'Christus' (Winchester Cathedral) by P. E. Ball, 1987. (Photo: Roger Twigg)

'Crucifixion' (In a private collection) by P. E. Ball, 1985. Beech on oak with metal additions, 76.2 x 66 cm (30 x 26 in)

Altar cloth (with twelfth century wall paintings above,
in Holy Sepulchre Chapel, Winchester Cathedral) by Alice Kettle, 1993.

'Risen Christ' (Liverpool
Anglican Cathedral)
by Elisabeth Frink, 1994.
(photo: Carl Fox)

'Archangel Gabriel' Icon
(Winchester Cathedral) by
Serguei Fedorov, 1992.
Tempera on lime wood. (Photo: Michael Call

'Crucifixion' (Church of
Notre Dame de Toute Grace,
Assy, France) by Germaine
Richier, 1949/50. Made of metal.

'Crucifixion' painting
(St Matthew's Church,
Northampton) by Graham
Sutherland, 1946.

icon, a niche for a bust, six lampstands, a communion rail kneeler; in 1994 a process began at York Cathedral and was not wholly resolved at the time of writing in respect of a medieval figured surround at the west door, much worn by weather and vandalism. Questions under consideration were: should it be left as it is? Should a new figured surround replace the present one which would be preserved in a museum? In this case should the Genesis story of the original be copied, re-created or should another story be sculpted? If the present figured story is to be kept should it be corrected or left in its present illogical condition? At Southwell Minster a new West Window is under consideration, designed by Patrick Reyntiens and the architect Martin Stancliffe, glass to be made by Keith Barley.

We note again that there is plenty of activity in English cathedrals, not only in terms of maintenance, but also in terms of embellishment. The problem of quality remains. Bearing in mind the amazing medieval achievement it is doubtful if many additions to our cathedrals merit their place. The CFCE/FAC mechanism is not devised to provide the best. It is in place to prevent the worst and monitor whatever is proposed.

Two difficult cases are worth mentioning in some detail as indicating that the inevitable tensions between conservation and new creation may not always be resolved. In 1990 a committee was formed at Winchester Cathedral to consider the possibility of renewing virtually the whole of the Cathedral textiles: vestments, robes, carpets, kneelers, banners and altar linen. With few exceptions the existing textiles were worn or mediocre or inappropriate in their fitting or environment. Quite a number came from ecclesiastical furnishers. The project manager, Anne Sutton, MBE, combined an excellent aesthetic eye with a wealth of experience as a weaver and judge of textiles at international competitions. She had written a number of books on the subject and completed her merits with a discreet and patient manner. The Visual Arts' and the Crafts' officers of Southern Arts acted as consultants, the Precentor and I completed the committee in its initial ordering.

About 15 artists were engaged, chosen for their excellent work and the likelihood that they would relish the commission. No questions were asked about their religious beliefs, but in the initial meetings in the cathedral an historical and theological account was given of the place and the project. This included written documentation. Each artist was introduced to his or her task, had the resource of the Cathedral library and personnel at hand, and were asked to produce a design. Since the general tradition of design in ecclesiastical textiles is unimpressive, in contrast both to the splendour of the *Ordo Anglicana* of medieval times, and the contemporary secular achievement, no detailed brief in respect of colour, material or iconography was determined. We had faith in the artists and in the language of the Cathedral. Conversation did, of course, occur. The curator and I were not infrequently asked questions of a historical or theological nature. Our hope was that existing pieces would be preserved in a Cathedral textiles' museum and that we would assist the much-needed break-through in quality of textile work for English churches. We engaged Issey Miyake, the renowned Japanese clothes' artist, so that vestments and robes might be re-thought in purpose, shape, colour and weight.

The FAC questioned whether so large a project could be assimilated at once and intimated that the re-furbishing of one chapel at a time might have been a more appropriate method of procedure. In our method we had endeavoured to see the Cathedral as a whole but to avoid uniformity by engaging different artists who worked simply at their own task. Each artist accompanied his or her design with a written description of their intent. A site meeting with members of the FAC and a delegation from the CFCE was held in the Cathedral. A few designs gained assent, enthusiastic praise even, most, however, were reckoned not to blend with their environment. Some existing textiles were considered still serviceable and of historic interest. A Comper dorsal portraying the crucified Christ was so designated. Some of the proposals were felt to be unconvincing in themselves. A report to the Commission was understandably highly critical.

The corporate view of the Commission was expressed in ameliorated tone, clear evidence that it was trying to meet local endeavour as far as it felt able to do so. It expressed itself as follows: 'It was agreed that advice to the Dean and Chapter should constitute a general note of encouragement, whilst stressing that a more holistic approach was necessary. The relationship of each design, both to its immediate setting and the rest of the building, should be carefully considered, as should the need to retain and conserve some existing textiles. It was also decided to recommend that each design should be the subject of an individual application to the Fabric Advisory Committee, and that they should not be taken together as a single application.'[1]

On this occasion it seems obvious that there was a breach in cultural understanding between the supervisory bodies and the textiles' committee. Behind the textiles' committee lay the cultural understanding of more than a little of the textiles craft of England. This may be explained in part by the desire of the committee to see novelty and the desire of others to conserve. The CFCE procedural understanding whereby, having made its own judgement, it placed authority largely with the FAC must be praised for removing a bureaucratic layer and keeping judgement at the local level.

The CFCE defence of Comper's dorsal image of the crucified Christ focuses the breach in understanding, Comper has a place in the twentieth century history of ecclesiastical buildings and their furnishings, but some of us found his work nostalgic and effeminate, a Victorian inspired image of Christ, quite lacking the vitality Feibusch had pleaded for, that has done so much harm to Christians and unbelievers alike. On the question of holism it is worth saying that the textiles' committee conceived the project as a whole but that we were conscious of the fact that the cathedral is comprised of many different architectural styles and is in no sense a simple integrated building, such as Liverpool Anglican Cathedral.

---

1. CFCE minutes 1992

A most significant footnote is that the altar cloth by Alice Kettle, intended for the Holy Sepulchre Chapel had been largely made when, for a number of reasons the project as a whole was abandoned. We persevered with the design and the FAC and it was eventually accepted. The complete altar cloth can be seen in the Chapel today and the general public and those intimately involved in the life of the Cathedral seem to think that it blends beautifully. Alice Kettle's own statement, slightly revised for the FAC application, is worth quoting as it is a model in itself and shows how fully she let the reality of the Chapel communicate itself to her:

'My aim has been to complement the artistry, imagery and technique of the medieval wall-painting in the Holy Sepulchre Chapel.

In wall-painting, paint is applied to plaster, giving strong bright colours in places, softer tones where the paint has been absorbed into the plaster, and white areas where the paint has come away with the passage of time.

In keeping, my frontal is stitched much as a painter applies paint: layer upon layer of different thread, with tones and shades frequently re-defined. The background is white and silver, a translation if you like of plaster into thread. Soft pastels produce a tone both impressionistic and contemplative. An occasional bold brush stroke reflects the strength of colour of the original wall paintings, and lends a gently contemporary note.

But most importantly I have concentrated on gold thread. Traces of gold paint have been found on the angel wings on the East Wall of the Chapel, whose paintings date from the 1160s. And gold thread imbues the frontal with a quiet, majestic glow.

In terms of visual design, this strength is also suggested by the symbolism of the pyramid. The attentive eye will notice a progression upward, from the solitary figure on the frontal, through the Deposition scene, to the Pantocrator above, Christ in Majesty.

Another device I have used is to draw the gaze of the viewer from outside the Chapel through the open arch and into the intimacy of the Chapel by continuing the legs of Christ around the near side of the altar.

If the decay of time and death is one impression of the Chapel, then hidden strength and majesty is surely the underlying statement. I have sought to hint at this mystery, and to complement these beautiful paintings in my own medium of thread.'[1]

If we compare this statement, and the completed altar cloth in its designated place, with the recorded view of the CFCE even the most sympathetic person must recognise the possessive sensitivity in respect of old things and the innate hesitancy in respect of the embellishing new things, that committees weighted in favour of conservation sometimes engender. Almost by accident a splendid textile was won for the Church, token of that break-through in aesthetic excellence for which some of us yearn. An added irony in this Chapel is that another, almost illegible Deposition wall-painting adorns the west wall, having been transferred there from the east wall where it covered the present painting. We are reminded that the medieval mind approached the significance of decoration in a much less fraught way than ourselves. But for the sake of preserving the past we have been prepared to overturn liturgical propriety by having the same scene on the small chapel's two main walls, and liturgically meaningless fragments transferred to yet another wall.

A second example will confirm the view that those who would embellish old depleted buildings may encounter unreasonable opposition from authorising bodies. Antony Gormley, 1994 winner of the Turner Prize, and widely recognised as one of England's best sculptors donated his fine lead sculpture *Sound II* to the Dean and Chapter of Winchester Cathedral on the condition that the site for it in the crypt was sufficiently prepared. The gift was offered just before the CFCE/FAC structure of oversight came into being

1. Author's Archives

and it remains an unanswered question whether this sacred piece, which blends easily with its eleventh century environment would have been approved by the current authorising bodies. Gormley was attracted to this site because an ancient well can be found in the central aisle, so that water is always near. Furthermore, for about three months in the year water floods most of the crypt almost to knee height. Water, used in baptism, fundamental to the earth, symbol of life, is important for the sculpture, which both contains it and has water cupped in the hands of the figure. Gormley has evolved as an artist through the experience of Roman Catholicism, study of anthropology and archaeology, and Indian culture. The parameters of his artistic perception lie somewhere between Catholicism and Buddhism. In this sculpture the notes of contemplation, mystery and the threshold point of spiritual awareness are all richly evoked. But the evocation depends upon a delicate attunement between sculpture, environment and viewer. As we look across the water towards *Sound II*, we glimpse beyond in the shadow the Romanesque arches that lead into the mystery of the unknown but trustable further shore.

Obtruding into this environment at ground level is a stub of unoriginal wall about 122 cm (4 feet) long and 61 cm (2 feet) high. It must have been once part of a dividing wall, later removed and the stub left incongruously behind. The arrival of the sculpture gave prominence to the stub of wall. The sculptor, the architect and the Dean and Chapter wanted the stub removed. The architect submitted a letter for the authorising committees which described the stub as 'obtrusive' and went on to allege that 'as the wall was once an intervention in the history of the Cathedral so now is the sculpture and its presence lays new emphasis on the physical appearance of the crypt aisle and the quality of the space'.[1] A letter to the same committee was written by the sculptor, saying that 'when the crypt is flooded the sublime resonance of this calm, level, in-door sea which extends into

1. Author's Archives, 25 Feb. 1993

areas of the crypt which are not visible is disturbed by this remaining vestige of masonry'.[1] The Dean and Chapter and some members of the FAC suggested that the wall should be removed, recorded and kept so that it could be replaced if necessary.

The Cathedral Archaeologist saw the matter otherwise. In his letter he recognised the aesthetic desirability of removing the wall but believed it was unnecessary. The artist had accepted the location and he should remain satisfied with it. The stub remaining permits useful conjectures respecting the history of the cathedral.[2]

The decisive view of the CFCE was that it is 'wholly inappropriate for a part of the historic fabric of the building to be demolished solely to provide a particular setting for a new piece of sculpture. Agreed unanimously to refuse application.'[3] The strong word 'demolished' indicates the emotion felt by the Commission. This case tests the argument that the authorising bodies are weighted in favour of conservation and we may reverse the intention of Morris' eloquent question, quoted earlier, that our learning has become a snare for us.

George Pace (1915–75), one of the most eminent cathedral architects of the last generation, was very conscious of the threat to our ecclesiastical heritage by the very structures now making their presence felt. He wrote, 'the petrification of the type all too often adopted by the ancient Monuments department of the Ministry of Works of the buildings and ruins in its care, or the approach to the Cathedral and Church maintenance by the State in, say, France or Denmark, have no place in the maintenance of English cathedral and church … It cannot be too greatly emphasised that the scarcity of money and the immense missionary and economical possibilities which surround the raising of restoration funds are tremendous safeguards against the fate which overtakes so many

---

1. Author's Archives, 9 June 1993
2. Author's Archives
3. CFCE Minutes, 29 July 1993

continental cathedrals and are bulwalks against the growth
of the National Monument or the museum conception of
the Cathedral.'[1]

The Clergy and Education

Cultural conditions apart the key to a revival of exemplary
practice in the creation and decoration of churches must lie
with the clergy. Bishops lead the Church and are immensely
influential. Parish priests lead in the parish and their influence is locally pervasive. Let us consider briefly the educational assistance ordinands and clergy receive to increase
their awareness of the importance of this subject. I begin
with my own record since I am a clergyman. I have taught in
theological colleges for fourteen years, and I was responsible
for continuing ministerial education in one diocese for nine
years. As an ordinand I do not recall any lecture on sacred
visual art, nor was our student body ever formally introduced to the visual splendour of the Cathedral about which
the college had its campus and in which we worshipped
weekly. In post-ordination training and in continuing ministerial education the subject was never addressed. As a
lecturer and an organiser of clergy education sacred visual
art was never on the agenda. A Roman Catholic doctrine
lecturer of my acquaintance illustrates her lectures with
slides drawn from the heritage of painting and sculpture.
This intelligent device which does not call for extra
curriculum time never crossed my mind – but what a graphic
(literally!) educational means it must be.

In 1977 the sculptor Edward Robinson sent a questionnaire to 200 randomly chosen Anglican clergymen born after
1940, enquiring how far the development of their religious
feeling or understanding has been influenced by the visual

1. P. Pace, *The Architecture of George Pace*, p. 126, Batsford, 1990. It is interesting
to observe that in the list of recipients in the Queen's Birthday Honours, 1994, no
awards were given for creative work in churches. Conservation, however, is well
represented: Jennifer Page, Chief Executive of English Heritage, a CBE; Claude
Blair, CCC, an OBE; Richard Butler-Stoney, Vice-President Norfolk Churches Trust,
an OBE; John Howard Doyle, President Romney Marshes Historic Trust, an MBE.

arts. 168 sent no reply. 6 informed Mr Robinson that they had nothing to say. 15 said they had been hardly influenced at all. Among the remaining 11 (5.5% of the total) most had been touched by traditional Christian art, one or two showed some appreciation of modern art. In a postscript Mr Robinson adds that the Institute of Religion and Theology listed 1300 dissertation titles for 1976. 8 came under the heading 'Art and Architecture'. Only one of these deals with art in any deep or wide sense.[1]

In January, 1992, I circulated a questionnaire to the Principals of the 14 Anglican theological colleges in England. There were nine replies; most were perfunctory; one, from an Anglo-Catholic college, was considerate. The results may be summarised as follows:

Question	Answer: Yes	Answer: No
–Visual art in formal curriculum	5	4
–Visual art in informal curriculum	4.5	1
–Reputable visual artists involved in embellishing college chapel	0	8
–Would prospective students be attracted to college if visual art was part of curriculum?	1	6
–Books bought for college library on visual art, 1990–92:	2 bought none	
other numbers:	30, 20, 10, 10, 6, 1–2	

–*Other comments*: students encouraged to visit museums and exhibitions; artist in residence funded for one term (Richard Kenton Webb); students opposed to Christian dance and drama; chapel banner to be made in-house; one student known to favour a college emphasising visual art; –ecclesiastical awareness of visual art reflection of general cultural position; one college would like to fund an artist in residence; most colleges mentioned crowded curricula and limited budgets.

1. Author's archive

In October 1994, I circulated questionnaires to diocesan officers in the Church of England responsible for post-ordination training and continuing ministerial education. 42 Questionnaires were sent and the replies, all of them considerate, may be summarised as follows:

(A) POST-ORDINATION TRAINING

Question:	*Response:*
Courses on sacred visual art in last 5 years.	– 32 replied. 1 had 10, 1 had 4, 1 had 2 2 had 1, 27 had 0.
Titles.	– e.g. icons and calligraphy in relation to spirituality; Art and Theology: Resaissance Masters; visit to Iona and study of Celtic art.
Sacred visual art as component in allied subjects.	– 31 replied. 5 included it, 26 did not. 1 will begin in 1995.
Clergy requests for course on sacred visual art.	– 31 replied, 29 negative 2 positive.
Importance of sacred visual art for Director.	– Very important 4; important 5; not important 21.

(B) CONTINUING MINISTERIAL EDUCATION

Question:	*Response:*
Courses on sacred visual art in last 5 years.	– 31 replied. 2 had 4; 2 had 3; 2 had 2, 1 had 1; 24 had none.
Titles.	– e.g. Christian symbols for 2001; Prayer and Painting; Study tour to Italian cities, with preparatory course; listening to the World of the Artist.

Sacred visual art as component in allied subjects.	– 31 replied. 3 included it; 27 did not. 1 will begin in 1995.
Clergy requests for courses on sacred visual art.	– 31 replied, all negative.
Importance of sacred visual art for Director.	– Very important 3; important 7; not important 23.

Anyone who believes that visual art is a language parallel to the verbal and that is is capable of channelling the divine to man, must find these tables, crude as they are, very disappointing. Two points seem very likely to be true; first, that the general culture of which Christian culture is a part is not particularly conscious of the significance of visual art. Second, that theology is understood largely as a verbal and logical discipline. This is consequent upon our culture being largely verbal and logical in its educated members. The Reformation supplanted a visual with an aural culture, and the Church has been responding verbally and logically to verbal and logical attacks upon its claims. It is the argument of this book, however, that sacred visual art is important for the Church and it must be thought odd that courses on liturgy rarely include the subject specifically since liturgy is in part a visual communication.

We may compare the foregoing statistics with some from English Roman Catholic seminaries. I sent a questionnaire to the four Roman Catholic seminaries in England in October 1994. The results may be summarised as follows:

Question:	College 1	College 2
Visual art in formal curriculum.	Only visual setting of mass in Middle Ages.	Occasional visits to V&A workshop on art in worship and theology.
Visual art in informal curriculum.	Depends on personal interests.	

Reputable artist(s) involved in embellishing college chapel.	Chapel re-ordered 1978 including vestments.	3 or 4 works of art commissioned in in last 5 years.
Books bought for college library on visual art, 1991–93.	24 or so.	6 or so.
Do seminarians have any perception of the importance of the subject?	Yes, but not enough.	Yes, but not enough.

Roman Catholic understanding seems little different from that of Anglican.

If a Roman Catholic parish wishes to commission a major work of art for its church it contacts the Diocesan Liturgy Commission's Art and Architecture Committee for advice. Good practice would involve the Commission's interest at every stage. The provision of vestments and altar cloths is left to the discretion of the parish priest who must work within the norms laid down in the liturgical books. In further letters of explanation the Chairman of the Portsmouth Catholic Diocese Liturgy Commission said that the Diocesan Liturgy Commission had no formally distinct Art and Architecture Committee. He mentioned two local Catholics, one an architect and the other a sculptor, who assisted when required.[1]

In the General Instructions of the Roman Missal (1975) we read that chalices should be made of non-absorbent material and that 'The artist may give a form to the vessels which is in keeping with the culture of the area and their purpose in the liturgy'. Among the numerous instructions respecting vestments it is stated, 'The beauty of a vestment should derive from its material and form rather than from its orna-

---

1. Author's archive, 27 Oct. 94; 3 Nov. 94; Fr A. Griffiths, Portsmouth Catholic Diocese Liturgy Commission

mentation. Ornamentation should include only symbols, images, or pictures suitable for liturgical use, and anything unbecoming should be avoided. Colours in vestments give an effective expression to the celebration of the mysteries of the faith … On special occasions more noble vestments may be used, even if not the colour of the day.'

The purpose of visual art in churches is to heighten awareness of the sacred according to the revelation of God in Christ, and to support the liturgy. Michael Jones Frank, a Roman Catholic liturgist, has observed, 'There has been at work a twentieth century form of iconoclasm, a reduction of liturgy to words and rite alone. On the other hand, artists are producing highly creative works of Christian art, but so many of these are difficult to see as having any relevant place within the context of public worship.

The rite of the dedication of churches in the Roman liturgy witnesses to the symbolic nature of the church building, The Church, the liturgical assembly is understood as the heavenly city, the true temple. The church-building is understood as the image of the assembly. The building is not merely a shelter, but is an integrated structure taking its shape from the liturgy, consisting of all that goes to make it up as the image of the holy city, with its furnishings, artworks, devotional artefacts as well as its architectural features, the icon of what the Church is in its essence.

Liturgy is multi-dimensional. Liturgical artwork is as much an integral part of the liturgy as is music and song, as much as the drama that unfolds at the altar, as is the word of God.'[1]

It is natural to think in consequence that in the absence of a special Commission of the General Synod, the Liturgical Commission would include consideration of the subject in its brief, or be in close relation with the CCC and the CFCE on this matter. The recently retired Chairman of the Litigurical Commission wrote to me as follows: 'The functions of the Liturgical Commission are to prepare forms of service at the request of the House of Bishops; to advise on the experimental use of forms of service and the development of the

---

1. *Church Building*, January/February, 1995, p. 15

liturgy; to exchange information and advice on liturgical matters with other churches both in the Anglican Communion and elsewhere'. During the Chairman's time encouragement was given to the setting up of diocesan liturgical or worship groups, and to the inclusion of liturgists in DACS. Although 'artistic matters did not formally come on our agenda ... We did try to ensure that there was liaison between ourselves and the RSCM (Royal School of Church Music) and the Council for the Care of Churches'[1] The present chairman recognises the difficulty of trying to integrate liturgy, art and music as the Roman Catholics do, but he works in this direction. So far as visual art is concerned, 'I think the Church is still woefully inadequate'.[2]

In answer to an enquiry I sent to the secretary of the Winchester Diocesan Worship Group we read, 'You raise an interesting point about the Group's agenda. We have not specifically addressed the subject of visual art in sacred places. This is not because it would not be an appropriate area to be within the brief of the Group. Its low profile has been because of the Group has been reactive rather than proactive and the demands made upon the Group have majored on words and music. This has also reflected the current composition of the Group, which is strongest in liturgists and musicians. We have been urging links with the DAC, and have a representative of the DAC on the Group ... It is a subject that deserves a higher profile than the Group has so far been able to give it.[3]

It is difficult to think that the institutional recognition of this subject is as strong as it ought to be. If the Liturgical Commission and Diocesan Worship Group were able to include sacred visual art within their briefs quite specifically, and formal links between the Liturgical Commission and the CCC and the CFCE, and the Diocesan Worship Groups and the DACs were strengthened a more adequate response would surely be made to worship and sacred buildings. For

1. Author's archive, letter by the Lord Bishop Colin James to the author, 24 Nov. 1994
2. Letter of Bishop David Stancliffe to the author, 25 1994, author's archive
3. Author's archive, Letter from the Revd Dr Anne Barton to author, 24, xi, 1994

this to happen effectively it would be important to include visual artists and/or art historians in the committee work. Inter-disciplinary seminars should also be important for the Church has something to learn about the possibilities of sacred art, as well as something to practice.

Since the Reformation, and more particularly since the Enlightenment, the general movement has been for creative visual art and churches to lose their former close association. In recent generations expert and energetic steps have been taken to heal the rift between the Church and music and the Church and the conservation of its own buildings. Such expertise and energy are found only sporadically where sacred visual art is concerned. An acid test lies in the use of money. The Howe Report *Heritage and Renewal* contains useful analyses of Cathedrals finances. The expenditure analysis of all English Anglican cathedrals reveals:

Upkeep & Fabric	£10,554,000
services, music, choirschool	£4,605,000

No direct mention is made of the creation of visual art, here or in the more detailed figures in appendix 5, though there is recorded Library/Archives and Upkeep of Precinct/Gardens and the grants made for specific purposes. It would seem that creative work in the visual arts receives little recognition except where conservation is involved. This reflects the constricted mentality of the times. It is significant that the Howe Report, which is intended to be a major state-ment guiding cathedrals in their present activities includes no chapter on visual art and the sporadic remarks it makes are unmemorable.[1]

Canon David Bishop, who is a qualified architect and vice-Chairman of Art in Churches, a body founded partly by Walter Hussey, which for 15 years has been concerned to advise and make grants for the visual embellishments of churches wrote recently, 'The sadness is not the paucity of new works in churches today but the paucity of the quality of so many. That is a matter we are continually trying to

1. See the critique J. Halliburton (editor) *Cathedrals and Society* (1995)

rectify. The employment of artists not necessarily within the orbit of the Church serves to enlarge its vision, whereas the established ecclesiastical artist generally has not – or is not given – much vision of the Christian faith in visual terms. He or she will often produce works which are both aesthetically and theologically unsatisfying, and which fail completely to communicate visually with the world, for which the Church exists.'[1]

This chapter can only end on an ambiguous note, ambiguous because it tells against bureaucratic authority, ambiguous in another direction because it tells in favour of creative talent. The Rector of St Stephen's Walbrook in the City of London in the mid-seventies to the mid-eighties was the Revd Chad Varah. His Churchwarden was Peter Palumbo, soon to be made Chairman of the Arts Council. Palumbo was given charge of the restoration of this magnificent Wren church. He and Varah were convinced that the conception of a church as an auditorium was outdated and that the idea of the community of the faithful gathered abut the Lord's table was much more apposite. A new altar was required and Palumbo suggested the name of Henry Moore. Responding to the invitation and brief Moore recommended a central, round stone altar resting on the floor like a moulded rock. The altar would be light in colour, the surrounding pews light beech wood against the dark wainscoting. A faculty was applied for and the problems of the case meant that it was heard eventually in the consistory court. The petitioners were represented by a Queen's Counsellor who was also Chancellor of several dioceses. The Chancellor of the court refused the application on the grounds that the proposed altar was not an altar within the meaning of the Act as it had no legs, and that it was incongrous with Wren's architecture. The intrepid petitioners appealed to the Court of Ecclesiastical Causes Reserved, consisting of two High Court judges and three bishops. The Appeal was granted. Completion of the major restoration of the church, with the new altar in place, was celebrated at a

1. *Church Times*, 28 January 1994

special service presided over by the Bishop of the diocese, who consecrated the altar. In his sermon the bishop made no mention of the Restoration Fund Committee, nor the Lord's Mayor's encouragement of his parish church in its work, nor the patrons of the Appeal and Grocer's Company who had contributed so much, nor Christopher Wren, nor Henry Moore, nor the architect, Robert Potter, nor the organ and choir: but he did commend the liturgical use of the Book of Common Prayer![1]

The service took place in 1987, before the revised structures of oversight came into force. What would have happened today?

---

1. Chad Varah. *Before I die Again*, pp. 332–3; 355–6, Constable, 1992. Varah estimates that Palumbo is the greatest church benefactor this century.

3 The Significance of Sacred Visual Art

SISTER WENDY BECKETT has very usefully distinguished religious, spiritual and sacred art from each other.[1] Religious art is governed by the figures and doctrines of a particular religion, such as the persons of Christ or Mary, and it may or may not be spiritual or sacred. The Virgin and Child over which controversy raged at Cottingham[2] is doubtless a religious work illustrative of Catholic belief, more Roman than Anglican. Christians who perceive Christian truth in the terms represented in this image will be able to focus their thoughts and feelings on God in its presence and therefore will value it. A Catholic of any denomination nurtured on the writings of such contemporary theologians as Kung and Rahner would not be able to value it; nor would most Anglicans and Protestants.

A spiritual work of art may or may not represent what is representable in a particular religion. It is not a simple translation into paint or stone of a holy person or doctrine. It is more deeply felt and the subject has been more deeply considered. A spiritual work of art is an act of creation. It is not simply a repository for our piety, it touches us at a dimension deeper and more living than encapsulated formulae and superficial emotion. A spiritual work of art will arrest us, prize open doors in our minds and hearts, and bring us into relation with a world beyond the ordinary. The landscapes of Constable and Turner, the apples of Cézanne and the interiors of Matisse offer well known examples of spiritual art. These works are not religious but spiritual. When we consider the Conversion of St Paul or The Descent from the Cross by Rubens we are contemplating religious art that it also spiritual. Rubens was a master artist and a believing Catholic. He was pleased to work in the service of the Church and of the Counter-Reformation. His work is deeply impressive.

1. *Art and the Sacred*, Introduction, pp. 2–8, Rider, 1992
2. See Introduction, pp. 1–2

Sacred art is simply spiritual art that has become transparent to the numinous. It is a figuration of Being, created by an artist who is in relation with Being. Sacred art evokes a sense of the sacred in the sympathetic viewer. Its range is narrower than that of spiritual art but it is the most intense depiction of reality. It may or may not be religious art. The paintings of Fra Angelico are sacred and religious art. It is said that when this holy monk painted crucifixions he wept. As a man he empathised totally with the subject matter of his painting, as a Christian he believed all that the Church said about this matter, and the Christian and the artist were one. Mark Rothco was a Jew believing no particular credal form. His style of painting was abstract. Many of his paintings, such as those which decorate the chapel at Houston, Texas, or Number 1, White and Red (1962), are sacred art. On a background of black there exists in this painting three modulated blocks of colour, brown at the bottom, then red, and finally white. Sister Beckett interprets, 'Rothco is making visible the perpetual context of all experience, the darkness of suffering, whether seen or not. But it is a pain capable of the most exquisite chromatic sensitivities, a redeemable pain, a pain that will lift us up to God if we will accept its mystery'.[1]

It seems to me that we cannot exclude any of these gradations in art from churches so long as they are religious or, in being spiritual or sacred, consonant with Christian belief. The appropriateness will depend on the siting and the expectations and aesthetic development of the priest and people. What must be added, however, is that mass-produced religious artefacts tend to the mediocre and even the tawdry. Their theology is usually conventional and dated and their appeal is to superficial emotions. It follows from this that a church alive to its visual responsibilities will be looking for work created by artists and craftspersons, carefully chosen and briefed, and thereafter left as free as possible. Other things being equal the very act of creation has in it a spiritual quality lacking in the mechanized production of a factory.

1. Op. cit. p. 124

Mention was made earlier of St Thomas's medieval understanding of beauty (p. 26). Beauty, he believed, is to be separated from goodness and truth. It requires wholeness, harmony and brightness. Abbè Suger, it will be remembered, had a more Platonic view (pp. 21–22). The Florentine Platonist, Marsilio Ficino (1433–1499) expounded this understanding, finding in beauty the splendour of divine light. Ficino united goodness and beauty and believed that they begin in God, that they are communicated to the earth and may be again re-united with God. He says that this process 'may be called beauty insofar as it begins in God and attracts to Him; love, insofar as it passes into the world and ravishes it; and beatitude insofar as it reverts to the Creator'. The descent of the 'splendour of the divine goodness' brings it division and corruption in this fallen world, matter especially polluting it. But the inherent unity and nobility of this goodness and beauty is never lost and keeps the creation in touch with God. In human experience beauty 'calls the soul to God', and Platonists often derive the Greek word for beauty καλλος from the verb καλειν 'to call'. The perception of beauty may be sensuous but it can rise to an enraptured contemplation above sense and reason. Artists on this argument become important, even priestlike, in their work, producing guides and points of inspiration for humanity.[1]

This Platonic view, however modified, seems to me nearest the truth in stating verbally the accomplishment of sacred art. If we say that God is the heart of being, that his eternal values are goodness, beauty and truth, we can see that, whatever perverting or dimming effect this fallen world has on the out-pouring of his grace, beauty and truth belong together, distinguishable but not separable, and that they carry marks of their divine origin. It is for this reason that mathematicians speak of the importance of beauty in formulating their theories and Mother Teresa of Calcutta understands her work of alleviating the suffering of the poor as something beautiful for God. Similarly, we notice that pain

---

1.　See E. Panovsky, *Renaissance and Renascences in Western Art*, pp. 184–8, Icon Edition, 1972

cleansed the soul of Rembrandt, leading to a change in his painting style and intensifying the manifestation of the divine in his later portraits.

Cecil Collins was one of the most important English sacred artists of this century. He spoke to me of the visions he occasionally saw with the eye of the heart. He could only describe the experience as a kind of rapidity to which he was sometimes attuned. This mystical reality was then filtered through his consciousness, his imagination creating images as mystic source and painterly expression interplayed with his personality to become recorded in paint on canvas. He believed that his paintings retained an aliveness which could make them a channel for the viewer to begin the ascent to God. Here are two extracts from his writings: '*Symbols are not things representing something else*, they are actual emotions of the reality of existence, realised in concrete form, that can be experienced'. And again, 'For the artist and the poet there exists a great zone of consciousness into which this cosmic drama is transmitted and reflected and enacted. This is the archetypal world to which the human psyche has access. This eternal archetypal world of original essence is again reflected into the world of time and space in works of art and culture and in moments of transformation of consciousness in the spontaneous experience of living, or during the canonic and ritual participation of religion.'[1]

The Christian claim is that the archetypes, whose origin is God, press upon this world; that they are reflected indeed in the great mythologies and religions of the world and that in Christ the central purport and drama was enfleshed. Through the eucharist, set in buildings appropriately decorated, with appropriate music to support the liturgy that archetypal world resonates with the archetypal essence in man. The historical manifestation was necessary since God is love. It was necessary also that the myths and archetypes should be clarified and discover their norms and right ordering. In

---

1. Ed. Brian Keeble, *Cecil Collins, The Vision of the Fool and Other Writings*, pp. 66–90; Golgonooza Press, 1994. Compare J. Polkinghorne, *Science and Creation*, pp. 75–6, SPCK, 1988 for a scientist's view.

respect of other faiths and mythologies the Church, in my view, does well to resist exclusive claims, which degrade true perceptions outside its range and all too often witness to psychological imperialism; to resist as well a pluralist acceptance of the variety of religious experience, since perceptions clash and quality is sometimes distinguishable, and to insist on inclusivism, whereby in principle truth is to be encountered in many places and forms, and Christ is understood as the animating power wherever truth is found, but that anything that is true can be brought into relation with the historical revelation recorded in the Bible. Involved in this consideration is not only a recognition of the incompleteness of non-Christian religion, but the incompleteness of the Church, which also needs to change and to grow.

The representation of these perennial forms will depend on the personality and belief system of the artist and be affected by the conditioning effect of the culture of which he is a part. In the case of Cecil Collins, for example, we have a sacred artist more gnostic than Christian, an artist who had difficulty in admitting the created world and the principle of incarnation. It is true also that religious art that is not sacred and spiritual and sacred art of any kind all witness with varying degrees of purity to the ineffable reality of God.

In his remarkable essay, *The Vision of the Fool,* Cecil Collins writes, 'The true priest is a fool whose purity of spirit is the folly by which the world grows and becomes enlightened ... The Saint, the artist, the poet, and the Fool, are one'.[1] Collins' concern is to acknowledge the virginity of spirit, paradisal awareness, new birth in God that characterises those whom he lists. Such persons are alive to the spiritual world and channels for that world's ingress into this world. Thus Oscar Kokoshka, from a slightly different perspective, said, 'The test of truth of such a vision or dream is its compelling visual reality, and that is why many merely academic allegories remain, in art, so deplorably unreal, simply because the artist has never been able to

---

1. Op. cit. pp. 76, 81

visualise them properly, to see and observe visions, with accuracy, with all the spontaneous emotional impact of a real experience.'[1]

Virginia Haggard wrote of her lover, Marc Chagall, whose ecstatic sense of the sacred knew no dogmatic bounds but who produced some of the finest Christian art of our century, 'Marc knew that there was some mysterious force working within him filling his paintings with dream forms, but he didn't feel a need to elucidate their origins, and it disturbed him when others tried to do so. He knew very well that they were charged with significance, but to his conscious mind they were purely arbitrary forms, elements that he used in the construction of his paintings, sometimes drawn from visible sources, sometimes from memories. He used them for their shapes, their colours and their mysterious greatness.'[2]

In the terms of this book it follows that the artist in the service of the Church is a minister of religion and a theologian. He is a minister of religion because what he creates supports liturgical worship and is part of that holy theatre we call the church building. He is a theologian because what he creates speaks of God and unfolds the logic of God. The Lesser Festivals and Commemorations in the Revised Calendar of The Alternative Service Book 1980 of the Church of England commends John Bunyan, Charles Wesley and George Herbert for their ministry through literary endeavour, but no visual artist finds a place.

Two witnesses of the power of sacred visual art may be quoted. Dostoevsky's wife records the effect of his seeing Holbein's Deposition in Basel Museum. 'He stood for twenty minutes before the picture without moving. On his agitated face was the frightened expression I often noticed on it during the first moments of his epileptic fits. He had no fit at the time, but he could never forget the sensation he had experienced in the Basel museum in 1867: the figure of Christ taken from the cross, whose body already showed

1. E. Rodit, *Dialogues-Conversations with European Artists at Mid-Century*, p. 78, Lund Humphries, 1970
2. *My Life with Chagall*, p. 102, Robert Hale, 1987

signs of decomposition, haunted him like a terrible night-mare. In his notes to *The Idiot* and in the novel itself he returns again and again to the theme.'[1]

Since art and the Church are for all people it is not amiss to quote my own experience, humble though it is. Cecil Collins was showing my wife and I some of his paintings, placing them on an easel to make viewing easy, and talking as he displayed. Looking at the Angel with Adam (1950), a glorious paradisal work in golds and yellows, with the angel, Adam, the tree of life and the sun prominently placed, I found myself out of ordinary time and place, included somehow in the wonderful living and present reality of what was depicted before my physical eyes. Amid this serene beauty the Angel entered me while remaining itself. After a while ordinary consciousness quietly resumed. Neither of my companions were aware of any change in my consciousness and I have no idea for how long I had been transported. I had been granted admission to a higher and better world and the radiance of which St Thomas writes were pervasive. But love and secret, that is unstateable, knowledge was granted. The experience constituted also some kind of call to high service and, but this is a rational reflection, I was being assured of angelic support.

The main purpose of the church building and its decoration is the celebration of the eucharistamid the community of believers. The design of the building and its decoration must facilitate this act with its various demands for the services of Word and Sacrament, priest and people, and such visual embellishment as will support and illustrate the eucharistic action. Some acts of worship will not be eucharistic, some gatherings will not be for formal worship, some individuals or small groups may be legitimately present who quietly walk through the sacred space or sit quietly. All these factors must be taken into account in design and embellish-ment. No design or system of embellishment is a necessary pattern but any design or embellishment must form a

1. Quoted D. Magarshak's Introduction to *The Idiot*, p. 7, Penguin, 1955. A lengthy description may be found in the novel. Pt 3, ch. 6

coherent part of the whole answering to the purpose of the building and decoration.

This means that abstract and figurative art are in principle admissible and a mixture of both may be inevitable and probably will be enriching. Whatever is there must fulfil canonical and practical purposes with elements that please, instruct and hopefully, heighten awareness of God.

The argument of this book affirms the Catholic and Orthodox vision rather than that of Protestants and Anglicans, prior to the Tractarian revival. I cannot see that the Bible and the early tradition of the Church negate visual images and I do see that it is natural to man to absorb knowledge and beauty through his eyes. The cutting words of R. S. Thomas, with a lifetime's knowledge of Welsh Nonconformity must be recalled:

'Protestantism – the adroit castrator
Of Art; the bitter negation
Of Song and dance and the heart's innocent
joy'. (*Song of the Year's burning.*)

Spirit and matter cannot and should not be separated. They are to be integrated, aligned according to the Spirit's motion. The permanent importance of Protestantism lies less in previous formulations than in an insistence that no form is final. There is, as Tillich taught, a God above God, forms of truth beyond our ken which when grasped modify what now we possess. Allied with this perception is the importance given to the personal encounter with God, and individual responsibility before him. Rembrandt is a Protestant artist and the note he strikes must be included in the medley of Christian art.

The artist, as creator and minister within the Church must be granted genuine freedom. Freedom is the liberty to do right, but the artist may perceive visual rightness better than ecclesiastics, art historians and art critics. Committees tend to compromise and compromise is the death of the creative spirit. Françoise Gilot records how Picasso received once a message from the art dealer, D. H. Kahnweiler, including a cable from artists and officials at the Museum of Modern Art in New York. The cable asked him for words of support in view of the mounting opposition to modern art and freedom of expression in art. The bourgeois mind linked such developments with communism, and communists linked it with bourgeois decadence. Picasso's response was immediate and decisive: 'art is something subversive. It's something that should not be free. Art and liberty, like the fire of Prometheus, are things one must steal, to be used against the established order. Once it becomes official, and open to everyone, then it becomes a new academism ... If art were ever given the keys of the city, it will be because it's been so watered down, rendered so impotent, that it's not worth fighting for ... Anything new, anything worth doing, can't be recognised. People don't have that much vision. There is an absolute opposition between the creator and the state ... People reach the status of artist only after crossing the maximum number of barriers. So the arts should be *dis*couraged not *en*couraged.'[1]

However partial or exaggerated Picasso's remarks may be, the thrust of them is correct. But the Church cannot turn away from the genuine artist because the artist, consumed by Promethean fire, has a role very like that of the Hebrew prophet, and the perfect fruit of the prophetic tradition is Jesus. Granted that, we cannot avoid recognising that inspired though the Church may be, it remains in considerable measure an institution. The legislation now governing the introduction of new art to churches has tightened bureaucratic control in an area where true freedom is crucial. Dostoevsky's Legend of the Grand Inquisitor, in which the thin-lipped ecclesiastic confronted Christ, returned to the earth, with the assertion that he was mistaken and asked too much of humanity, remains the classic imaginative context of any searching discussion on visual art in sacred places today.

Crucial in the ministry of the creative artist in the Church is the re-birth of images. According to Paul Tillich culture is the form of religion and religion is the substance of culture. It follows from this that Christian iconography will differ in

1. F. Gilot & C. Lake, *Life with Picasso*, p. 187, Nelson, 1965

its expression as culture changes. The sovereignty of God will be a concept easy to portray visually for the citizens of an absolute monarchy. Christ becomes an aristocratic Spaniard for the seventeenth century Spanish/Cretan painter, El Greco. The crucifixion and the imaging of Mary have differed in marked respects according to the culture, including the religious belief, of the period. Such change and variation are a sign of the strength of the Christian tradition. As indicated earlier the Incarnation, and the biblical record, are an event and writings that are intended in the providence of God to evoke a response and perhaps to create a dialogue as believer, historical fact and tradition encounter each other. Tradition develops as the old through the challenge of the new is re-born. The shock of the new sometimes prevents viewers from recognising the continuity in discontinuity in all authentic Christian development, which is always an unfolding of the original revelation through time.

The case of St Mary Magdalene illustrates the argument. The only sure historical knowledge we have comes from the four gospels. The evidence is fragmentary and contradictory. It seems, however, that Mary Magdalene was one of Christ's female followers; that she was present at the crucifixion; that she was a witness of the Resurrection (according to John she was *the* witness); that she was the first apostle charged with the supreme ministry, proclaiming the Christian message. The fundamental assertion is that Mary Magdalene was a witness of the gospel and an important woman among the first believers, since she is carefully named. Mark 16.9 refers to the seven devils Jesus cast out of her, but this final section of the gospel is an addition. Luke (8.2, 3) refers to the same exorcism but there is no implication of sexual sin. 'Magdalene' comes from a Greek source to indicate the Israeli village Mejdel, a habitation near Tiberius, notorious for its licentiousness, razed in the first century. But such a circumstance proves nothing, though it might start a rumour.

It seems that Mary Magdalene and other Marys in the gospel stories are sometimes confused. Luke tells of the woman who was a sinner (7.37f) and Mary of Bethany figures largely in St John's gospel (11.1f; 12.3) and is men-

tioned by Luke (10.39). There has been confusion about the
character of Mary Magdalene from the third century until our
own time. Pope Gregory the Great (d.604) reinforced the
confusion by declaring all these Mary's one and the same.
According to Susan Haskins Mary has been regarded as a
repentent whore from the sixth century until now.[1]

What is the artist to create if asked to portray Mary
Magdalene? In times past, due to honest literary confusion,
but also no doubt to a twisting of the evidence to preserve
male imperialism and emphasise the enormity of sexual lust
from a male standpoint, Mary was portrayed, perhaps as in
Donatello's powerful wood carving, as a fasting, penitent
hag or, as in numerous stained glass window designs by
C. E. Kempe, reflecting general medieval tradition, as a
gorgeous young woman, in resplendent robes and flowing
golden hair, kneeling at the foot of the Cross, embracing it,
with imploring eyes turned upward. The latter representation keeps its value as a metaphor of one human response to
the saving grace of Christ. Donatello's figure is a brilliant
depiction of a sub-Christian reality, for the gospel promises
release from sin, not endless sorrow for sin committed and
repented. But the figure of Mary Magdalene can at last be
freed from false shackles to embody either a malaised
person healed by Jesus or, more importantly in an age that is
recognising the equality of women with men and admitting
women into the priesthood and episcopate, as the first
apostle. In Grace Cathedral, San Francisco, Episcopalians
have done this, and a fine icon shows a strong vital woman's
face, her hand holding an egg, symbol of new life.

An artist faced with such a commission and those faced
with writing a brief for the artist have the difficult task of
confronting habitual thought with correcting evidence and
new perception. Those concerned with caring for a good
existing building must begin with what is there. The problems that this includes can best be addressed by considering
a classic case: the preservation of the West Front of Wells

---

1. See *Mary Magdalene*, HarperCollins, 1993. I am much indebted for information
about the tradition of Mary to this book

Cathedral. Most people qualified to make a judgement agree that the sculptured West Front of Wells is one of the supreme achievements of medieval sculpture, but the dilapidation of time, the shattering effect of religious dissention and the clerical neglect of heritage meant that by the mid-point of this century remedial action had become necessary. Too much was wasting away and loose fragments were in danger of falling on passersby.

A brief outline of the history of the West Front is as follows. The building of the Cathedral began in the 1180s and Bishop Reginald conceived it in orderly intimate terms, as the vaults and interior suggest. In the second decade of the thirteenth century, however, the mason of Bishop Jocelyn was in charge of developments at the west end, and he thought in terms no less brilliant than extravagant. A huge stone screen was wrapped round the west end, broader than it was high and ending on the east side of the two angle towers at the corners of the west end. Shafted tiers of decorated niches face the viewer outside the west door with space for over 400 sculpted figures in the niches. Most of these date from the period c1215–c1250 and they are of good or superb quality. 385 figures are distributed over nine tiers. At the centre and lowest level we find the Virgin and Child; above this we find the Coronation at the Virgin; at the top centre is Christ in Majesty. Between these extreme points and extending throughout the screen is a complex iconography founded upon a typological interpretation of the Old and New Testaments. The Christ in Majesty is the key to the whole. In their original state it appears that the sculptures were painted white, in red niches, with eyes and hair painted black and lips red.

During the Civil War the centrally placed Virgin and Child, and the Coronation of the Virgin above it were mutilated. Bodies were decapitated and hands were hacked off. At some later date the upper torso of the Christ in Majesty dislodged, fell to the ground, shattered, and was lost. Whatever sporadic repairs took place as the centuries went by in 1879 Gilbert Scott and Benjamin Ferry undertook a thorough restoration.

In 1967 the Dean and Chapter resolved to investigate the cleaning of the screen and sculpture. As a preliminary to this venture they decided to restore the three greatest, but badly mutilated figures of the Virgin and Child, the Coronation of the Virgin and the Christ in Majesty. Dean Edwards wrote to the Cathedrals' Advisory Committee on 16 January, but did not consult the Cathedral Architect. He outlined his plans and said that the Chapter was considering inviting John Skelton to repair the three central figures. He asked the views of the CAC on aesthetic and antiquarian grounds, stressing the Chapter's unhappiness 'that these almost liturgical figures should stand headless and mutilated on a building set up for Christian worship'.

The CAC replied on 21 January to say that whilst they were biased towards purist conservation they understood the liturgical significance of the three figures mentioned. They advised that the figures should be removed and preserved in the Cathedral museum for scholars to examine. The Dean and Chapter should find a sculptor 'sympathetic with the original work to carve fresh figures. Whilst it is generally important that ... an artist should speak frankly for his own generation', in this case, 'the men chosen must be willing to sublimate his own style to that of the original, without necessarily being imitative of it'. The CAC felt that John Skelton might be too 'stylised for what must inevitably be a very humble and anonymous work'. Arthur Ayres of the Royal Academy school was recommended and Michael Clark, FRBS, as an alternative.

On 12 August 1968, A. J. J. Ayres wrote to Dean Edwards to say that he had examined the Virgin and Child group of sculpture (not the Christ in Majesty, isolated at the summit as the CAC had recommended) and found that they were strong enough to hold the suggested restorations. He believed that the work might prove controversial and suggested that first he make models in clay so that agreement might be achieved before actual work was done. On 2 September he wrote to the Dean to say how glad he was that his work had been appreciated and that he had begun to make casts.

On 29 April 1970, Professor George Zarnecki wrote to Miss Judith Scott at the CAC to say that he had heard that 'some very drastic restoration of sculpture' was being carried out on the front of Wells Cathedral. New heads were being attached to headless figures over the doorways. He could not be certain about these reports but hoped that she would check the facts. On 6 May 1970, Dean Edwards wrote to Miss Scott to say that he hoped she would re-assure Professor Zarnecki and he outlined what was being done, including the carving in stone from clay models by Arthur Ayres. The additions would be attached to the wall, not to the figures which they 'renew'. In May Miss Scott wrote two letters to Dean Edwards, one mentioning that the CAC would be very interested to see the completed work of washing and poulticing the West Front and the other to say that she had written to Professor Zarnecki and 'he is now quite happy about it'. The heads were fixed towards the end of May 1970, and a Cathedral mason added minor portions to the sculpture and its setting.

In April 1973, a delegation from the CAC came to view the clay models fixed to the Coronation of the Virgin. Members of the Chapter, the Cathedral Architect, and the sculptor met the delegation consisting of Sir Peter Scarlet, Professor Carol Waite, Mr Marshall Sisson, David Varey, the historian, Spencer Corbet of the Royal Commission of Historic Monuments, Mr Mandeville, Miss Shirley Berry, of the Victoria and Albert Museum, and the Clerk of Works who was in attendance. After a site examination they retired to consider the individual sculptures and the care of the West Front as a whole. Different views were expressed: remove the figures; preserve them in a museum, and replace them with replicas; remove the lower portion of the Christ in Majesty and replace it with a whole figure; clean the West Front and repair generally. One member favoured allowing nature to take its course.

On 7 February 1973, Mark Girouard wrote an article in the *Architect's Journal* entitled *Let Wells Alone*. He said that the action of the Dean and Chapter was as if the Director of the British Museum had telephoned a friendly sculptor and asked him to run up some heads and arms for missing portions of the Elgin Marbles. The Virgin and Child had been fitted with new extremities, 'a winsomely sweet little head and arm for the Child and sausage-like fingers with a great slob of a head for the Virgin'. Mr Girouard continued, 'it is not so much the depressingly bad standard of the new work, as the idea of adding bits and pieces to sculpture of this quality at all ... the sculpture in its complete state is immensely moving; the nobility of the original idea still shines through'. Any restoration 'will be a lie'. He questioned whether the ecclesiastical exemption should continue for churches and what the principles of restoration should be.

Mr Girouard promised that a storm would follow and it duly began with a letter to *The Times*, dated 8 February 1973. It was signed by John Schofield (of the Friends of Wells Cathedral), John Betjeman, Alan Bowness, Keith Critchlow, Mark Girouard, Lord Grafton, Henry Moore, Roy Strong, George Zarnecki and others. It said, 'The completed restoration is, inevitably, a disaster, negating the rhythm and vitiating the deeply personal nature of the original carving.

Great sculpture continues to project powerful images despite mutilation – think of the Venus de Milo or the Torso Belvedere. It is restoration that most imperils it and frustrates our own ability to experience the original strongly and directly.

The Coronation of the Virgin is perhaps the most expressive and moving sculpture on the West Front of Wells and arguably one of the finest sculptural works produced in England. To add heads and limbs to it is as outrageous as it would be to start replacing the lost fragments of the Elgin Marbles.

Insensitive treatment of works of art has often provoked criticism in the past. Ruskin, Morris, Rodin and Epstein all appealed as we do now, for a mature acceptance of the ineluctible process of decay, a process which we can hinder by constant and careful tending, but never reverse.'

Dean Edwards commented: 'Theirs is a point of view. But we acted with the guidance of the Cathedrals Advisory

Committee, who suggested Mr Ayres. I am unmoved.'[1] The diocesan Bishop, Dr Edward Henderson commented, 'I approve most heartily of it. I am in full agreement with the Dean and Chapter's decision.'[2] Within days of the unleashing of the storm Dean Edwards, who had a bad heart, was dead.

Other interesting and instructive letters were written and only a few of these can be quoted. Dr R. D. Reid, a Friend of the Cathedral and a local historian, said that he found the work of Mr Ayres 'wholly beautiful' and that of Henry Moore 'terribly ugly'. He said that it was an afront to Christians to see the mutilated figures on the West Front and that the Cathedral must not become an 'ugly museum'. Mr Hugh Adams, an art historian, wrote about the bankruptcy of modern ecclesiastical art, referring not only to the West Front but to the anemic Virgin above the Lady Chapel and the toffee-like Crucifix in the north transept. David Peace, a glass engraver, quoted Epstein that 'no nose is better than any old nose' and said that when the sculpture was too worn it could be removed and a modern sculptor commissioned to create new work appropriate for the setting. These could be removed if necessary and if good would become part of the history of the building.

On 13 February, the Archdeacon of Wells wrote to say that much of what we see now of the Cathedral is Victorian restoration work; that on the West Front about 50 statues have been lost; that a number of others look like 'lifeless mummies'; that others are without arms or heads; that all but a few are grimy and soiled by pigeons. He addressed the central issue passionately. Three of the statues are 'of my Saviour himself. And here I have no doubts. It might be right to keep a mutilated image of Christ in a museum, or even, if you fear idolatry, to destroy it altogether, but it must be an insult to him to leave a headless image of him over the door of his church ... We were right to restore the Virgin and Child; we are right to have commissioned the restoration of

1. *The Times*, 7 Feb. 1973
2. *Western Daily Mail*, 7 Feb. 1973

the Coronation of the Virgin, we shall be right, when generous help comes our way, to restore the Christ in Majesty.'

The Cathedral Architect, Mr Alban Caroe, summed up the present state of affairs with notable generosity and stated that the West Front must be treated as a whole and that the historic and aesthetic cannot be divorced from the moral and pastoral.

On 4 May 1973, the *Wells Journal* reported a stormy meeting between Henry Moore and the local historian, Dr Reid and others, when Moore tried to block further restoration. Dr Reid reported that Moore was highly critical of Ayres work and Mr Schofield had used strong language. Moore held that all the renovations were wrong.

A watershed came with the visit to the Cathedral of another CAC delegation. In August 1974, they issued their report. They recommended that the Cathedral authorities work with Government and other specialists on the whole West Front. There should be a comprehensive examination, cleaning and photographing of the area. The additions of Mr Ayres to the Virgin and Child should remain, but the Dean and Chapter should not proceed with the proposed additions to the Coronation of the Virgin. The Dean and Chapter had said that the value of the Coronation of the Virgin depended upon its legibility. The same applies to the Christ in Majesty. If they speak to our society they speak of iconoclasm and religious bigotry. Twentieth Century Christians should try to amend this unfortunate situation. The CAC, however, believed the Coronation, whether legible or not in its mutilated form 'is of great spiritual value'.

Time moved on. A new Dean, an Appeal, work, including successful experimental work of cleaning and conservation, was undertaken and then the lower existing torso of the Christ in Majesty was removed to the interior ground of the Cathedral and David Wynne was commissioned to create a new Christ in Majesty. L. S. Colchester, Cathedral Librarian recalled, 'Dean Mitchell carried out three months research at Oxford, as a result of which he discovered Hugh of St Victor's description which seemed exactly to fit this gable, in which the figure of Christ was described as flanked by seraphim, as recorded by Isaiah; and the two upper quatre-foils at the corners were, he said, the "mouths of God" through which the "Word may go forth from the Majesty" to the ends of the world. David Wynne accordingly carved the six-winged seraphim as he conceived them, and left the upper quatrefoils deliberately empty.[1] Philip Venning, Secre-tary of the Society for the Protection of Ancient Buildings knew of the development and wrote to *The Times* to say that he would have preferred the battered original to have remained, though he recognised that there were artistic and theological arguments against this view. At best, however, the new image could only be a crude substitute, at worst, what Morris called 'a feeble and lifeless forgery'. The flanking seraphim were even more worrying for they were historically very speculative. There is no record of the niches containing sculpture and if they did it is very debateable what they looked like.

On 7 August 1985, the *Architect's Journal* assessed the programme of conservation. It was noted that Edwin Russell had created a replacement for Bishop Bubwith faultlessly. Simon Verity had created a seated king which was awkward and tentative. Derek Kerr had created a similar figure that integrated faultlessly. David Wynne's Christ in Majesty was now in place and it was described as drawing its strength from early twentieth century primitivism, but it was too severe and the seraphim were incongruous. Angels would have been preferable.

David Peace drew interesting conclusions in the 1989 issue of *Conservation Today*. Granted the problem of conser-vation, what should the Dean and Chapter do? He believed that art historians would favour preserving the West Front as long as possible, thus providing responsible trusteeship. The Victoria and Albert Museum staff and Building Research establishment would favour restoration combined with removing dilapidated pieces and their replacement with replicas. Others might propose minimalist preservation

1. *Wells Cathedral*, p. 50, London, 1987

hoping that applied science would provide a permanent solution one day. Others would support the technique of repair and consolidation pioneered by Professor and Mrs Baker. In practice a compromise had been achieved. Some figures are treated with new materials, some are replaced. Peace believed that a humble carver working on site may well produce genuine work in the spirit of the originals better than an artist–sculptor working away in his studio. All he reports of Wynne's sculpture is that it is not universally admired.

The case of the conservation of the West Front of Wells Cathedral proved a watershed in Anglican thinking and has affected a much wider heritage-conscious public. Some of the main points to emerge from it are that the future of great old churches cannot be left solely in the hands of Deans and Chapters or priests and PCCs. The mechanisms now in place were in part called forth by such examples as that at Wells, and in principle we may be grateful for them. Through these mechanisms most would agree that preservation with minimalist restoration should be practised for the sake of the irreplaceable whole. What should happen when notable gaps occur? Do we agree with Dr Reid and the Archdeacon of Wells that legibility is the key to appreciating the whole, or do we agree with Henry Moore that until some quite major gaps become inevitable the rhythm of the whole communicates profound feelings, augmented even by the weathered conditions? Was Dean Mitchell right to pursue speculative theories that resulted in the appearance of the seraphim? Was the Dean and Chapter bold or reckless in replacing the lower torso of the Christ in Majesty with a newly commissioned work, whilst preserving what is left of the original?

Certain principles of action can be stated, the application requiring always consideration of the particular case. The aesthetic, historic and religious cannot be separated. Reid and Moore have important points to make and since any interference can easily prove to be wrong, the caution of Moore's view is preferable. Because of the nature of his gifts the Moore type of person would be able to imagine the parts in the whole better than someone with the more precise and literalist mind of a local historian. Both cannot be pleased and so long as the Moore argument convinces it should be preferred. There is a general cultural need to re-discover sensuous awareness and it must be wrong to give way before those who express the limited aesthetic awareness of our day.

Replacing old statues with new is also problematic. Imitation tends to be dead and a new creation by a sculptor of equivalent power to those who made the best of the original scheme might prove a disjunction where harmony is required. Practice alone must point the way to the kind of somewhat anonymous sculptor working on site who can respond to the images about him and accept freely the constraints they place upon him.

Unless we can learn how to arrest stone decay a point will be reached when age has become decrepitude. At this point it seems to me that consideration should be given to commissioning the best sculptor(s) to create a new programme of work reflective of Christian truth as it is perceived today. An important theological consideration involved at this point is that everything born in time dies in time. It is part of Christian wisdom not to cling to what is disappearing and to welcome what might be born.

Incarnation was not simply an historical event 2000 years ago, decisive though that event was. It embraces the Providential preparations for the event and the life and reflection of the Church since that event. Whom Christ is we both know and seek to discover. No pious crystallisation in stone should make us idolatrous in respect of it. God is greater than any such crystallisation and seeks new forms of embodiment.

If it is said that such a response lacks clear rules the difficulty must be admitted. In life such is often the actual case. The moral virtue needing to be practised is that of prudence. R. C. Mortimer writes: 'Prudence first of all considers carefully ways and means. So far as human uncertainty of the future allows, it takes into account all circumstances and possibilities. With these considerations in mind, it determines what now is best or right to do. Having so determined, it commands that the action be performed.'[1] The exercise of prudence admits the difficulty of actual circumstance, seeks information and judgement, and insists on action.[2]

We come now to the crucially important question of the commissioning of new visual art for churches. It is significant that in recent years the *Church Times* frequently devotes a quarter of a page to such new work or to exhibitions of ecclesiastical interest. Much of the work illustrated, however, is of a predictable nature; imitative of past traditions, kitsch, or badly made. There has recently been produced the Archbishops' of Canterbury and York's Commission Report, *Heritage and Renewal* (1994), which examines the role of English cathedrals in today's world. Much space is given, and rightly, to cathedral music, much space is given, and rightly, to conservation and the structures of oversight, but scarcely a word is written about the vitally important matter of commissioning appropriate new visual work. It is pertinent to remind ourselves that most people who visit cathedrals never hear music, but they are exposed constantly to visual art and, as in the case quoted earlier of Dostoevsky, visual art can affect the viewer with immense power.[3]

Some might argue that the presence already within the Church of a structure of oversight represented by DACs, FACs, the CCC and the CFCE means that expert advice is within reach of Deans and Chapters and PCCs, but there are various difficulties with this solution. First, these bodies are regulatory. They function best responding to proposals made to them rather than initiating new proposals. Second, if they warmly commend a particular artist their objectivity might be doubted if, for quite legitimate reasons, they rejected a

---

1. *The Elements of Moral Theology*, p. 225, A&C, Black, 1947
2. Most of the factual evidence about Wells cathedral was generously loaned by Caroe and Partners, Chartered Architects, Wells. I wish to thank Mr J. Sampson in particular
3. It commends the Cathedral group set up by the Liturgical Commission but sees no particular need for special help with visual art (p. 116). To say 'the care and repair of a cathedral requires a creative outlook just as much as its embellishment' (p. 115) is a complacent sentence, oblivious of the hierarchy of truth. It is purblind and bureaucratic to say that cathedrals should be able to help churches in the diocese through the DAC (p. 127)

proposed work by an artist not named by them. Third, political factors are inescapable. Consciously or unconsciously these bodies which, within prescribed limits, perform a valuable function, may wish to control conservation and innovation in our churches and cathedrals. The regional and national centralising effect of such control would stereotype even further the present unsatisfactory position and smother the necessary local truth of a particular church or cathedral. Fourthly, these bodies include among their membership devout Christians but since the criteria asked for are of a professional nature some members may be atheistic, agnostic or members of a non-Christian religion. Unless criteria were changed this could lead to bizarre judgements on priority and symbolism for new proposals. Fifth, these four bodies, comprised of persons with differing briefs are subject, like all committees, to compromise and the persuasion of dominating personalities. Granted the history I have traced it is difficult not to think that a predominant concern will be the need not to aggravate Governmental ministers or the amenity societies in case grants are withheld or the ecclesiastical exemption removed. Such strong preoccupations are not the best preparation for judging good art. The experience of George Baselitz, the distinguished German painter, is worth pondering. Phillipe Dagen interviewed him and 'Baselitz got talking about the contemporary German art scene and a recent incident that had deeply shocked him: when he had donated a picture to the church (one of his series of crucifixions) there was such a violent controversy that the priest who had accepted the gift received death threats.

'There you have German society, which lacks structure and authority. It's a total democracy – which is less and less cultured ... Even within the Church – despite its anti-democratic nature – every worshipper has his say. With a system like that Michaelangelo wouldn't have been allowed to paint the Sistine Chapel.'[1]

1. *Guardian Weekly*, 25 September 1994

Lastly, these bodies are heavily biased in their membership towards tradition and conservation. It is the working of
such factors that explains the kind of decisions reached
where significant modern art has been presented for judgement and rejected or modified. Some of these cases have
been mentioned in our earlier discussion.

What is required is what was suggested by Bishop Bell
forty years ago, the appointment of a visual arts' officer in a
diocese or between a small group of dioceses, possibly, but
not necessarily a residentiary canon, who proves his ability
to point parishes and cathedrals towards the best that
contemporary artists, able to work in a sacred environment,
can produce. Such a person will marry theological and liturgical knowledge with an interest in visual art, not least visual
art outside the orbit of the ecclesiastical institution. He will
try to develop relationships with appropriate officers of the
regional arts' councils and have recourse to the slide library
of the CCC, though this needs to be improved if it is to be of
practical use as a guide to excellence.

The procedure of choosing an artist may be in principle as
follows: if a PCC or Dean and Chapter have a person whose
judgement can be trusted, he or she should be engaged to
explore alternatives as best they can. Such an arrangement
allows full scope for the personal but avoids the eccentric
since formal contracts and committee agreements will be
essential before any commitment is given. It is worth
reminding ourselves that if the proof of excellence lies less in
procedure than in results, most of the brilliant commissions
in this century have taken place through the strenuous
endeavours of single-minded and illuminated individuals.
The word 'patron' means 'father' and such a word is full of
personal meaning. The best art is likely to be born where a
personal relationship of understanding and trust exists
between client and artist. Committees are less able to
fulfil the needed role than a sympathetic and knowledgeable
individual.

In two significant commissions where my personal role
was decisive a related but distinguishable factor was
involved. In the case both of the birth of Elisabeth Frink's

Head of Christ and the inclusion of Cecil Collins and Patrick Reyntiens in an ecclesiastical commission I had a revelatory experience regarding the work of each artist. Involved in this experience was the call to approach the artists and invite them to work for the Church. The dimension of truth expressed here is that of prayer insofar as prayer means communion with God. I am firmly convinced that each venture was God-willed and at the time I believed that they would be fulfilled, whatever obstacles lay in the path. If sacred visual art at its best is what I indicated earlier, and the artist working in the Church is a minster of the Church, then the dimension of prayer is clearly integral to the whole process of bringing into existence a sacred image. Most of us would associate committees with testing rather than realising the inspiration of a particular commission.

However this stage proceeds the point would come where names have to be considered. Advice should be sought from a diocesan visual arts' officer, the regional arts' council, the CCC/CFCE, or from any person or institution likely to be helpful. Examples of the artists' work by catalogue, portfolio, slides or photographs should be made available and site visits to see it in location where this is possible. The artist may be asked how they would approach the commission. Depending on how the commission develops a particular artist may be chosen or a short-list may be drawn up. The latter method suggests more openness and the surprise of an artist being chosen who may not otherwise have commended himself, but sometimes a particular artist for a particular commission will seem right.

The PCC or the equivalent body should agree the short-list and the artists should be invited to visit the site, talk about the proposed commission, meet members of the authorising body and be shown the brief, which has been ratified by the same body. In due time the artist may be invited to comment on the brief and it may be modified accordingly.

The artists should then be asked to submit a design or maquette, perhaps with an accompanying written statement. The authorising body should then choose the artist for the commission. The brief will have included the cost and method of payment and the timetable. The artist chosen should indicate that he accepts these terms and be advised of the other authorising bodies that may have to be satisfied with the proposals for the commission. Once permissions have been obtained it is important to trust the artist and to recognise that the finished work may differ somewhat from the design. Creativity must be granted a degree of freedom. At each stage between inception and completion the congregation should be kept informed and shown evidences of the developing work. This educative process can be important for the artist as well as for the recipient body.

The installation of the new work of art should be marked by a ceremonial occasion, normally an act of worship with a dignitary to unveil it. This occasion should be pervaded by a sense of joy and accomplishment.

In their important enterprises of engaging artists to work in the service of the Church, the Church is exposing itself to the world of art and of artists. Such is the separation between the enterprises of religion and of art that something should be said about art in our time. Clearly if art is to regain a measure of its old relation with religion and bridges are to be built between the two enterprises it is important that there is mutual understanding. My impression is that there is a large degree of ignorance on both sides.

The Russian-American, P. A. Sorokin, sometime Professor of Sociology at the University of Harvard, wrote a remarkable book in 1940, called, *The Crisis of Our Age.* My personal views run along the same lines as his and more importantly his general thesis is affirmed by such writers as Theodore Roszak, Cecil Collins, Herman Hesse and James Joyce. Sorokin believed that human culture tends to follow a recurrent pattern. Ideate culture is one where concern for the divine is primary and overwhelming. Idealistic culture is one where the divine is recognised and may be predominant but man and the world gain substantial recognition. A sensate culture is one where the divine is no longer acknowledged and where mundane concern predominates. This latter phase is unstable, due to a loss of the sense of the divine, and a culture moves into either an idealistic or ideate phase once more. Sorokin believed that we live in a sensate culture and that it has entered its unstable phase. His thesis is substantiated by a mass of statistics and the interested reader is referred to his writings for details.

Analysing 100,000 pictures and sculptures drawn from eight European countries he discovered the following trend (in percentages):

Period:	pre10c	10–11c	12–13c	14–15c	pre16c	17c	18c	19c	20c
Religious	81.9	94.7	97.0	85.0	64.7	50.2	24.1	10.0	3.9
Secular	18.1	5.3	3.0	5.0	35.3	49.8	75.9	90.0	96.1
Total	100	100	100	100	100	100	100	100	100

As regards the styles by which the arts work were produced he analysed:

Style:	pre10c	10–11c	12–13c	14–15c	pre16c	17c	18c	19c	20c
Sensate	13.4	2.3	6.0	53.6	72	90.6	96.4	95.5	61.5
Ideational/ symbolic	77	92.2	51.1	29.2	20.3	5.9	2.5	0.3	0.7
Expressionistic	0	0	0	0	0	0	0	2.8	25.5
mixed	9.6	5.5	42.9	17.2	7.7	3.5	1.1	1.4	2.3

Sorokin's conclusion is that the sensate culture that has governed Europe for the last five centuries is over-ripe and is breaking up. It has become increasingly hollow and contradictory. Trying to please the market reduces its vitality; recording appearance rather than essence breeds sterility; desire for sensation diverts from the normal to the flashy and eccentric; desire for novelty leads to loss of balance and coherence and all such needs lead to the worship of technique. Instrumentality becomes an end and sensate art develops into an art of professionals leading to the separation of the artist from the community. Sorokin sees Modernism as a revolt against sensate art on sensate art's own terms. Our period is provisional. Ideate or idealistic art will supervene.

However much we may doubt the exactness of Sorokin's statistics there does seem to be substantial truth in his thesis.

In the last hundred years one style of art has superceded the last with unnerving rapidity: academic, impressionist, post-impressionist, fauvist, vorticist, futurist, analytical and synthetic cubist, dadaist, surrealist, expressionist, pop, op, social realist, neo-romantic, anti-art and the rest.[1] The influential English painter and critic Roger Fry, declared that art is Significant Form, an aesthetic pattern without reference to the world beyond the picture frame. Lawrence Alloway, the biographer of Roy Lichtenstein, the renowned pop artist, described his subject as not only including comic motifs in his art but 'Viewing comics as a continuum of shared values'. He goes on to say that the group of artists of whom Lichtenstein was one found their problem to be 'to produce art without metaphysical sanction. Timelessness was contrasted to topicality, other worldliness to quotidian life.'[2]

Francis Bacon was one of the mid-century's most important painters. He is immensely popular with critics and therefore with dealers, collectors and the viewing public. Bacon was an atheist and could discover no meaning in existence. He regarded art as a 'game'. According to his biographer, Michael Leiris, his art 'is a ludic activity conveying no message'.[3] Those who may have been exposed to much of the work of Bacon may doubt this evaluation. Bacon's contemporary and polar opposite, Cecil Collins, discerns the reality beneath the intellectualised veneer. Bacon 'paints Hell, and Hell is a most popular subject today because so many people are in it'.[4] This means that Bacon is a metaphysical painter. He was conscious of the absence of God and his painting reveals the landscape of godlessness; futile, distorted and pained.

1. Eduard Vuillard's biographer relates, 'He certainly believed that as a result of the rapid turnover of opposing "isms" there had been a woeful loss of direction in contemporary art and criticism, and that artistic success had become simply a matter of luck. If an artist remained true to his convictions he would have to harden himself against wild fluctuations in taste and critical response' (B. Thompson, *Vuillard*, p. 147, Phaidon, 1988)
2. Roy Lichtenstein, pp. 40, 42
3. *Francis Bacon*, p. 6, Thames and Hudson, 1988
4. B. Keeble, *Cecil Collins, The Vision of the Fool and Other Writings*, p. 133, Golgonooza, Press, 1994

The discoveries of Collins in his artistic vocation were quoted earlier. (p. 109). Whether or not we accept the vocabulary through which he expresses his experience he finds himself figuring Being, seeking to express the ultimate harmony and order of the universe. From such beatitude and coherence modern art is largely separated, suffering the agony of loss or accommodating to the diminution of vision entailed in a sensate culture. Typical of our time is the action of Lee Krasner, artist and wife of Jackson Pollock, who transcribed some words of that most modern of poets Arthur Rimbaud on her studio wall:

> 'To whom shall I hire myself our?
> What beast must I adore?
> What holy image is attacked? What hearts shall
> I break?
> What lies shall I maintain? In whose blood tread?'

She identified with Rembrandt's dismissal of mere beauty, his belief in the absolutely modern and attempt to discover truth by voyaging into the depths.[1]

A consequence of this cultural dislocation is that artists have an environmental dissuasive from pursuing the sacred in art. Those who bravely do so, usually suffer neglect or isolation. This was the case with David Jones and Cecil Collins in the recent past and with Margaret Neve and Albert Herbert in the present.

Picasso and Chagall sometimes are named as the two greatest twentieth century painters. Virginia Haggard pertinently observes 'No other painter has shown us the chaos of our era as did Picasso. Chagall gave a glimpse of the mysterious equilibrium that has always existed beyond chaos, that he believes might one day triumph over it'.[2] Part of Picasso's popularity is explained by the argument of this chapter. Chagall's popularity is explained, despite his essentially sacred perception by his unusually attractive lyricism, colouring and world affirmation.

1. P. Wood, F. Frascina, J. Warris, C. Harrison, *Modernism in Dispute*, p. 153, Open University
2. *My Life with Chagall*, p. 103, Norbert Hale, 1987

The neglect of the sacred artist is not simply the purblind quality of a sensate culture. The manifestation of the sacred rebukes those who live contrary to its beauty. The light of that beauty illuminates the squalor of unredeemed life which recoils from the revelation. The sacred artist finds himself in a situation similar to that of the Hebrew prophets and Jesus, who were rejected by those unwilling to face the challenge of prophetic truth.

The disregard for the sacred in a sensate culture is bound to include art colleges. The following statement from lecturers in the subject at the Open University may be typical: 'The characteristic pulse of our culture does not run through this or that radical movement, this or that style of art, even this or that political leadership. A case can be made for saying that it is to be found rather, in the commodity, in the commodification of everything, including art, and politics, and ultimately people'.[1] A post-graduate student in the history of art at one of England's leading art schools told me recently that the tradition of art was taught with scant regard for what the sacred must have meant in an earlier culture and that when she proposed researching sacred art in churches for her doctoral thesis only her insistence gained the subject's acceptance. As a teacher in important art institutions for many years the testimony of Cecil Collins is interesting: 'I was teaching metaphysical ideas, and very often only a few students would come and would often make a tremendous row and walk out of the class or shout insulting things. But all that's over now, now it's exactly the opposite way round. It's one's colleagues one's got to deal with now, not one's students'.[2]

Such an attitude seems to be maintained through much of the elite of the art establishment. Writing recently in the *Spectator*[3] Giles Auty reflected on the summer exhibition of the Royal Academy, lamenting the poor quality of many of the exhibits and the curious means of selection. He specified

1. Op. cit. p. 241
2. Ed. Brian Keeble, *Cecil Collins*, The Vision of the Fool and other Writings, p. 139
3. 18 June 1994

a particular example. 'The week after the summer show opened, I examined an almost life-sized sculpture of the Holy Family carved in lime wood by a virtually unknown young artist, Arthur de Mowbray. It was one of this year's many hundreds of outright rejections from the summer exhibition yet I do not think any current academician could have exceeded the skills it demonstrated. In a year in which much of the sculptural entry is unusually awful, this piece could hardly have been faulted for its almost medieval intensity and sincerity. Among those interested more in modishness now than morality, perhaps the real fault of the piece lay in its subject. While calves or dead sheep in preservative are worshipped on bended knee regularly now by art's more fashionable folk, I presume an image of the Holy Family must be regarded as peculiar or irrelevant. It must be apparent that the Royal Academy does not care much for everlasting- or even life-lasting values. For one thing it is too desperate trying to keep a foothold in the latest fashions.'

In a sensate culture the thirst for novelty and commercial reward augment each other with a tendency to seduce the artist. In his fascinating book *From Manet to Manhatten,*[1] Peter Watson traces the progress of the auction house and concludes that it links price to value, seduces artists and governs taste. As the poorer groups in society become more wealthy so pop art comes to be regarded as good art. Chagall was aware of this problem and spoke passionately about it, thus: 'our views are dictated by fashions and hypnotic fascination, also by the money value of a work of art. The critics, whose work it is to observe the fluctuations of an artist's life, to criticise, guide and stimulate, are often in league with the dealers. They work to promote, not to criticize. Critics like Charles Estienne are rare today. The dealers have made a hugely successful business out of the artist's absolute necessity to express his new vision, but if he becomes too affected with his success on the art market, he may never rise to anything timeless.'[2]

1. Vintage, 1992
2. Virgina Haggard, *My Life with Chagall*, p. 104, Robert Hale, 1987

All such evidences are suggestions of the truth of Sorokin's thesis. From the standpoint of art they also suggest one important reason why the Church and the art establishment are estranged. It would be a mistake to conclude from this that awareness of the transcendent and belief in God are concepts foreign to the artists of this century. Some of the more distinguished names include Jacob Epstein, Henry Moore, Barbara Hepworth, Graham Sutherland, John Piper, Eric Gill, David Jones, Cecil Collins, George Baselitz, Pierre Bonnard, Rodin, Frink, Balthus, Henry Matisse, George Braque, George Rouault, Maurice Utrillo, Marc Chagall, Gwen John, Mark Rothco, Robert Natkin, Kandinsky, Brancusi, Paul Klee, Emil Nolde, Ernest Barlach.[1] The father of modern painting, and possibly the greatest modern painter, Paul Cézanne, regularly attended mass and confessed, 'If I did not believe, I could not paint'.[2] It is some token of the estrangement of the Church and the visual arts that so many of these great artists were never asked to work for the Church. The few that were asked produced some of the most memorable sacred images of the century.

The Church made some use of Marc Chagall, but the institution's ponderous hesitancy was evident even here. Chagall was obsessed with the idea of painting large religious works. Having seen the Giottos at Padua and the Fra Angelicos at Florence he looked for a specially constructed building to house them. The Chapelle des Penitents Blancs belonged to the parish of Vence, but it was not used for services. Chagall's representations to the parish priest to use it were met with polite hesitations. The Chapelle du Calvare in Vence was also more or less abandoned but his request was met with the same disguised rebuff. Chagall's mistress Virginia Haggard, discussed with Père Couturier the possibility of painting biblical murals in a religious building and she suggested a temple that would embrace all mystical philosophy. Couturier icily rejected the view. In 1973,

1. See many references Alexander Liberman, *The Artist in his Studio*, Thames and Hudson, 1988
2. Op. cit. p. 6

however, without the help of the Church the Message Biblique Museum was established in Nice.[1]

The case of George Rouault is deeply instructive. Michael Ayrton pronounced Rouault the greatest living artist[2] and as names begin to be sifted into their hierarchy of excellence we may imagine Rouault's will be among the great ones of our century. The creator of the Miserere plates, the Apprentice Workman (1923), The Old King (1937) and the numerous Pierrots, Joans of Arc, Fights into Egypt and the Holy Countenance (1933) makes visible wholly Christianised archetypes. His contemporary lack of recognition is due to nothing other than a sensate culture being unable to perceive the hidden splendour of sacred art. A recent exhibition of his paintings at the Royal Academy chose work from the earlier part of his career and critics affirmed that his later work was sentimental and repetitious Nothing could be further from the truth. Rouault's first engagement was with the dark side of human life: prostitutes, corrupt judges and condemned men. His later work lightened as the sun of grace penetrated his vision and canvas. Our kinship with the earlier work makes it more acceptable.

But what employment did the Church give to this Catholic master, who attended mass daily? As he approached the age of 70 a panel of stained glass by Rouault was displayed in Paris, admired by Père Couturier, and included in the Church at Assy, to be followed by four other stained glass panels. Rouault received no further ecclesiastical commissions. Ecclesiastical displeasure settled on the great achievement at Assy and Rouault could only have painted as the ecclesiastical hierarchy wished by prostituting his genius. Such wanton neglect of talent says little for the Church and little for the art establishment. If it is true that the Church needs the services of the gifted visual artist to refresh its life and assist the re-birth of convincing images, and if it is true that visual art as a secular enterprise risks disintegration from lack

1. Virginia Haggard, *My Life with Chagall.* pp. 124–6, Robert Hale, 1987
2. In 1946 an article appeared in *The Spectator*, quoted by M. Yorke, *The Spirit of Place*, p. 23, Constable, 1988

of vision what can be suggested, mainly from the Church's standpoint, as a programme of renewal?

The urgent need is for education, education of the mind in terms of knowledge of the tradition of sacred art, not least the change of imagery through the centuries, and education in terms of increasing awareness of visual reality. Such education must include ordinands of all denominations. The chapels where they worship should express the thinking and vision of contemporary liturgy and sacred visual art. Sacred visual art must be allowed to take its place as a component in liturgical studies, ordinands should be encouraged to visit art galleries and particular exhibitions. In recent years splendid exhibitions in London have displayed the work of Pugin, Eric Gill, Michaelangelo, Cecil Collins, George Rouault and Russian icons. Lectures in doctrine and history may include pertinent slides, of the way, for example, the differing portrayals of the Crucifixion through the centuries witness to changing beliefs. Parish placements should include the possibility of keen ordinands being exposed to churches and incumbents that illustrate exemplary practice in this field.

The CCC should be encouraged to continue its conferences where sacred visual art and artists and potential clients can come together. The CFCE and DAC should be encouraged to include education for cathedrals and local churches. The CCC and CFCE acknowledge the importance of governmental and other bodies relating to this area of concern. They should be encouraged to make even more imaginative use of the opportunities that they have. With few exceptions the quality of speaker and exhibit lack the quality required if the gap between art and the Church is to be healed. Those in charge of clergy and lay education in dioceses should be encouraged to include courses on this subject in their annual programmes. The recognised importance of liturgy opens this possibility quite naturally. Commissions of the General Synod such as the CCC, the CFCE and the Liturgical Commission should be asked to review their membership to ensure that visual art is recognised as part of the concern of the particular commission.

The appointment of deans and canons to cathedrals should include a representation of those few proficient in this field.

A second urgent task is the process of appropriate commissioning. Something of the procedure has been considered already. We think now of its inner reality. The first consideration relates to context. Will the proposed new piece blend with its environment? Will its presence embellish the church and increase support for the liturgy? If the church is the kind that is visited much by the public can the new proposal affect them appropriately as well as the congregation on Sunday? The question of context relates to the material, colour and texture of which the piece will be made in relation to where it will be placed. It relates to the height, volume and visual projection of the piece in its surrounding. If the client has discovered a good artist this factor will normally be addressed. John Piper, for example, renewed the stained glass in the nave of the pre-Reformation church of St Margaret's Westminster. His abstract work harmonises perfectly, however, because he allowed his creation to grow out of and relate to what was about it whilst remaining true to his twentieth century inspiration.

The question of the quality of the projected new piece is naturally crucial and it is the burden of these pages that churches and cathedrals generally fail the test. Great care must be taken to select the best artist for the work and if necessary a church should wait rather than entrust a commission to an artist about whom legitimate doubts can be entertained. Where significant work is under consideration I believe that the distinctions made earlier between religious, spiritual and sacred art should be borne firmly in mind. The individual creative artist is almost always to be preferred to the ecclesiastical furnisher and religious art that is not spiritual is properly to be abhorred.

In considering finished paintings which may guide a church or cathedral to commission the painter to create a painting for them, or enable a church or cathedral to decide whether or not to retain a particular work in their possession I follow the divisions in assessment proposed by Jane

Dillenberger.[1] By extension this analysis applies to other forms of visual art. It should be remembered of course that some are blessed with the kind of perception that immediately assesses a work and analysis would seem to them foreign. Despite their different backgrounds Père Couturier and Robert Natkin are both of the intuitive kind.

Iconograpy. This refers to the subject matter and its representation. Is the painting abstract or figurative? Do the figures relate to each other? What is their dress and expression? How do buildings, clouds and landscapes relate to the whole composition? If the work is symbolic do the symbols convince and suggest the formal subject of the composition?

Composition. This refers to the pattern of the painting seen as forms and colours, not as persons and doctrines. It may be divided into:

Line. Consider the vertical, horizontal and diagonal lines. How do they relate to each other? Do they give overall balance and intensity? Where is the focus?

Rhythm. Lines convey rhythm. Is the rhythm slow or fast, placid or violent? Does the rhythm convey a lifegiving quality to the viewer?

Mass. Mass is enclosed by lines. The mass may be monumental, round, square, liquid, broken or small. In Rouault mass is often monumental. In David Jones it is usually more slight.

Space. Line and mass enable the artist to treat space. The shape of the canvas may be square or oblong (horizontally or vertically) or it may be circular. This affects the impact of the whole composition. The way the artist treats perspective, if at all, is crucial.

Light and Shade. Highlighting or darkening a part of canvas will suggest the presence or absence of sunlight, important and unimportant parts of the canvas or moral qualities in the figures represented. Rembrandt and Caravaggio were masters in their use. In Cecil Collins' paradisal paintings light is level and pervasive because darkness has no place there.

1. *Style and Content in Christian Art*, pp. 16–28, SCM, 1986

Meaning. This is bestowed upon us by the whole work of art. We are to receive it on its own terms, abnegating our egos, and releasing ourselves from the cultural conditioning that so often blinkers our outlook. The highest aesthetic moment is when we are one with the canvas and this may become a mystical moment.

If the Church will pay the price of renewing its concern for visual art in sacred places there is no reason why what has been accomplished at St Matthew's, Northampton, Coventry Cathedral, and the Church at Assy should not become more common. Given the chance there are many artists willing and able convincingly to work in the service of the Church. The consequence of the improvement for which we look will be to release visual art in our churches to communicate the sacred and the gospel to the habitual worshipper and to the visitor. It will be for the Church to develop its mission in a cultural domain from which it has been for too long estranged. Part of that mission will be to receive wisdom from the artist and another part will be for the art establishment to relinquish some of its inhibitions and recover an ancient and glorious association. Most of all it will enable glory to be born into a world where glory is obscured. The day will be hastened when a dying sensate culture will be transformed into an ideate or idealistic culture. In a metaphysical age humanity may prosper.

4. Exemplary Modern Practice

Whilst exposition has an important place in the deliberation of our subject, it is most of all by exposing ourselves to the works and lives of sacred artists that our awareness will be increased and we will recognise the enormous importance of sacred visual art in the ministry of the Church. Briefly, we will consider four modern artists, one dead, three living: Cecil Collins, Peter Eugune Ball, Margaret Neve and Albert Herbert.

CECIL COLLINS (1908–1989)

Cecil Collins was a Cornishman proud of a Celtic heritage that has given us such art and mysticism as we find in the Book of Kells and the poetry of Edwin Muir. As a boy he imbibed a live biblical religion from his mother and a natural mysticism in a wood near his parents home. He discovered 'the language of stones and grass and especially a white cloud that played a great part in any life later on. It seemed that cloud was a gateway to paradise. It was moments like this that came together and formed a kind of unconscious certainty that what we normally see is a very contracted and superficial view. The divine reality should be felt everywhere, in an insect, in an ant, in a fly on a window-pane, in a speck of dust.'[1] According to Patrick Reyntiens who was a friend of Collins and worked with him as a colleague at the Central School of Art, London, Collins was arguably 'the most important metaphysical artist to have emerged in England since Blake'.[2] The art of Collins was admired in his lifetime by such discriminating judges as Henry Moore and Kenneth Clark but it was only towards the end of his life that the Church gave him what he had long desired, commissions

1. Ed. B. Keeble, *Cecil Collins, Vision of the Fool and other writings.* Golgonooza Press, 1994
2. *The Tablet,* 27 July 74

to create sacred art in holy and public places. It was at the same belated time that the art establishment made him a Royal Academician and invited him to hold a retrospective exhibition at the Tate Gallery. Collins died soon after its opening. The prospect had probably kept him alive, not out of vanity but because, in the spiritual battle of his life, such recognition testified to the social triumph of the Spirit.

Collins excelled as a student at the Royal College of Art and, in 1931, married a fellow student, Elisabeth Ramsden. Their union produced no children but during their lives together she remained his support and inspiration. Though transformed it is her eyes that appear in many of the faces he drew and painted. His art and philosophy quickly matured so that two of his paintings were included in the acclaimed International Surrealist Exhibition, held in London in 1936. He broke with the surrealists almost immediately, however, for his stated and typically articulate reason that he believed in 'sur-reality'.

Collins was a visionary and a natural Platonist finding easy kinship with the images of ancient mythology and the symbols of man's universal religious quest. He read widely in these fields and was sometimes surprised to discover an image he had illustrated in an ancient text. Kathleen Raine rightly sub-titles her excellent monograph on Collins 'Painter of Paradise'.[3] He stands in the tradition of Blake, Palmer, Martin, Jones and the earlier Spencer, Nash and Sutherland in being open to the mystery of the Eternal in time and partly conscious of its undefined but vivid lineaments. He explained to me once that angels live at a more rapid velocity than we do normally, but that sometimes he gained their speed and beheld them. The oddity of his metaphor relates to the impossibility of verbal description. Collins believed that the being of God and the celestial world are imaged in a dimension of creation obscure to our normal consciousness which can nevertheless be penetrated by mystical perception. This higher world has its home within us and about us but it is usually overlaid and atrophied by

3. Golgonooza Press, 1979

mundane busyness. Those who penetrate to this dimension of reality express their discoveries in the perennial philosophy. In the Christian tradition we think of such writers as Dionysius the Areopagite, Meister Eckhart, Jacob Boehme and the later William Law. Collins had knowledge of these writers and explorers, as also of eastern mysticism and European sages like Goethe. I believe that some commentators have overstressed Collins' academic achievement. His intricate intelligence was not primarily scholarly, rather, scholars and sages cleared his mystical perception and prepared him for further discoveries. In the eighteenth century sense of the term his theology was essentially experimental.

The highest and most appropriate function of art for Collins was to express in visual images this intangible, paradisal life and recurrent images found their place in his work: the Fool, the Woman or Anima, the Angel, the Stream, the Sea, the Mountain, the Tree, the Chalice, the Moon, the Sun. Thus he continued the universal spiritual tradition that has given humanity dancing Krishna, the Genesis Tree of Life, and Dostoevsky's Idiot. Such images, rendered in paint or pencil, were not for him dead representations but living symbols, pointing beyond themselves and partaking in the life to which they pointed. These icons were for him comprised of the colour and tone of the paint as well as the shape of the figure depicted. Collins believed that his paintings drew their energy from that dimension of existence he had glimpsed and were able, for the attentive beholder, to transform his consciousness through the power of that higher dimension. He explained the nature of his art in the catalogue for the 1959 Whitechapel Gallery exhibition: 'I am not very interested in what is called "pure painting", or *objets d'art*. I am concerned with art as poetic consciousness, or as metaphysical experience. A picture lives on many levels at once: it cannot be analysed or anatomized into single levels because one level can only be understood in the light of others. The reality or inner life of the picture can only be realized as a total experience, and this totality, for me, is poetic consciousness. Single level experience, partial experience, like aestheticism, for example, seems superficial.

'If the subject in a picture is unimportant, we may well ask: unimportant to whom? The subject of the Crucifixion unimportant to Grünewald? To Fra Angelico? The themes on the front of Chartres Cathedral unimportant to its builders? The subject unimportant to Rembrandt? To Goya? The question whether a subject is important or not is for the artist to answer. Some subjects are a necessity to certain artists; others not.

'If we reduce the creativity of the artist to a mere aesthetic activity, if the idea of pure painting, pure art, is true and painting is nothing but an arrangement of colours, forms, textures, lines and qualities of pigment for their own sake, the be-all and end-all, then in our civilization this places the artist as a mere manufacturer of visual confectionery, a tickler of our surface senses, a not very interesting entertainer, which is where a cheap materialistic society living on appearances and substitutes would probably like to keep him. Pure art is the prettier side of the utterly empty mechanical desert we call modern civilization.

'The terms "pure art", "pure painting" seem to me to be meaningless. For me, colours and forms are instruments; and I hold the instrumental view of pictures as stations of transmission. In my experience, painting is a metaphysical activity. All my pictures are based on a theme, and the theme is the cause of all the forms and colour harmonies and no colour or line exists for its own sake. The subject is the context of forms and colours.'[4]

An artist with such a philosophy was clearly set against the cultural stream of his time and it is a tribute to Collins' tenacity and the clarity of his vision that he did not founder or drown. Not that he was entirely without success. Work was purchased, even by the British Museum, the Victoria and Albert Museum and the Tate Gallery. Exhibitions did take place, even at the Whitechapel Gallery and, as his life ended, at the Tate Gallery. Notable commissions by the Church were granted him eventually at Chichester Cathedral and at All Saints' Church, Basingstoke, but the neglect

4. W. Anderson, *Cecil Collins*, pp. 86 & 95

and misunderstanding of his art was constant and deeply wounding.

Collins showed equal mastery in most mediums of visual art; oil, gouache, water colour, drawing, charcoal and lithography. Technique was explored endlessly. In oil paintings, for example, he returned in later life to the study of the glazes of Rembrandt and he quizzed Cambridge chemists about chemicals and their interaction. He conducted his own experiments to discover how to glaze with the depth, subtlety and finish that we find in his later small works. In mid-life he could cooperate successfully with textile workers to produce magnificent tapestry and in old age he worked with Patrick Reyntiens to create stained glass worthy of a great tradition.

Our artist has stated in several places that, despite his profound reverence for Christ, and his recognition that the deliverances of his own soul were echoed in the dogma and ritual of a Catholic form of Christianity, that religion was today as tribal as any other religion claiming absolute truth. A consensus among religions with the recognition that despite particular emphases and vocabularies the essence of mankind's communion with God is a universal vision is what we must strive to realise in sacred art no less than in other forms of sacred communication. What might a Christian response be to what is widely felt by artists awakened to spiritual truth?

First, Collins was an artist of remarkable creative energy and spiritual perception. He had less need than most people for the rituals of a public institution as his inner universe was so alive. Worship calls to remembrance, but what is to be remembered was normally already in some measure present for Collins. Further, Collins was an introvert, whose inner sensitivity and richness led him to distrust public bodies, where compromise, defined truths and authoritative regulations prevail. Anderson compares Gill and Collins and concludes that Gill was primarily a craftsman and Collins, though superbly that, primarily an imaginative artist. Gill needed the institution to provide what his inner self lacked, but Collins, ever creative would, in previous centuries, have been a candidate for burning.[1] We acknowledge the bravado of this statement but it is unconvincing. The specifically artistic edge of Gill's genius has been increasingly recognised in recent years and the point of institutional constraints is that they purify and direct eccentricities to which everyone, not least the imaginatively fecund, are prone. Personal foibles apart the gnostic, anti-sacramental notes in Collins' vision are surely points, whose source lay partly in temperament and physique, and which ecclesiastical institution may have helped to correct. It is worth comparing the case of Collins with that of Blake who, whilst probably a Christian, rarely went to church. T. S. Eliot has commented upon the cranky nature of Blake's poetry, noting his lack of Catholic discipline. 'What his (Blake's) genius required, and what it sadly lacked, was a framework of accepted and traditional ideas that would have prevented him from indulging in a philosophy of his own, and concentrated his attention on the problems of the poet.'[2]

Second, the movement in Collins' vision is from the visible to the invisible. In typical Platonic style the ordinariness of created things is little valued and their glory little seen. But just as institutions correct individual eccentricities so the physical counter-balances the spiritual. William Temple relished the fact that Christianity is the most materialistic of all the great religions. For Collins this fact would have constituted its limitation. He spoke to me once about parenthood, expounding the view that the mother was simply the carrier of a new life that is essentially quite separate from her. A woman present grimaced and did so because of her intuitive recognition that mother and foetus, mother and infant, have very much a shared life and that the physical is not only the conduit of the bond between them but part of the bond.

Constitutionally and by conviction Collins was hardly capable of valuing the Incarnation. He believed that the myths and traditional religious philosophies were enough to

1. *Cecil Collins*, p. 42
2. *Selected Essays*, p. 322, Faber & Faber, 1951

suggest the love and power of God. But more of his own vision had been fed by the Incarnation and its consequences than Collins realised. His Christian upbringing and the fragments of Christian culture amid which he lived affected his perception. The sacramental vision of David Jones prepared Jones much more generously to value the enfleshing of God. The gnostic limitation of Collins' vision can be stated also as a failure to appreciate fully community, Good Samaritan-type action and the created world. Just before typing these words I saw and heard on television news of a Los Angeles black community worker who was helping homeless people, and made himself homeless so as to do his work well. He said he was doing a Gandhi act. Gandhi made himself untouchable in order to touch the untouchables. This is the Christian philosophy in a sentence. It is not a sentence we read clearly in the paintings of Cecil Collins.

Third, despite the foregoing Christ does figure in Collins' work and echoes of the chalice, the Cross, seen often in the shaping of a tree, the Trinity, seen often in the grouping of flowers and leaves, are quite common. His three drawings, the Agony in the garden (1956), the Crucifixion (1952) and the Resurrection (1952) are not only works of art of world class, they are among the most moving depictions of their subjects created in this century. His Angel Paying Homage to Christ (1952) and Christ before the Judge (1954/6) show a deep preoccupation with the person of Jesus confirmed in conversations I have had with Collins over the years. His late Walking on the Waters (1986), not only by its title but by the iconography of a central holy figure in a mandorla, flanked by fishermen and shapes that are both wings of the central figure and boats for the fishermen, suggests that the preoccupation remained. Enthusing one day on the imaginative writings of J. R. R. Tolkien, Collins responded by informing me that he had read little of the author and certainly not *Lord of the Rings*. He felt that the closeness of his and Tolkien's vision might adversely affect his own perception. Tolkien, however, was a deeply committed traditional Roman Catholic. His marvellous epic simply tells the Christian story in imaginative form.

' Reviewing the work of Collins when specifically Christian iconography is apparent Anderson comments, 'Alas, no deans and chapters, no devout millionaires, no humble priests, poor themselves but skilled in raising funds for the adornment of their churches, came in deputation or singly to Cecil Collins at this time to say, "You have shown us truths about our Lord and master that lay unknown in our hearts. Paint us something new so that the message of inner freedom that we try to preach, and fail to communicate, may strike our congregations and our visitors with the greater power of art". Something like this was to happen much later in Collins' career, but it was more than a shame that this particular vein was not explored at this time: it was a great wasted opportunity.'[1] The argument of this book indicates clearly enough why the opportunity was wasted, but the waste must have been an additional reason for Collins' disparagement of the Church.

At this point it may be worthwhile considering in some detail one of Collins' most powerful paintings where specifically Christian iconography is employed. The first version of *Christ before the Judge* was an oil painting completed in 1954. In 1956 Collins completely re-painted the figure of Christ. As Christ appeared first the body had a rounded form with a heart-shaped head echoed in the shoulders and chest. The figure is somewhat huddled. He is framed in the doorway of a tent and the lower edge of the entrance curtain to the tent moves in the breeze. It is the final version that will engage our attention.

The painting is large by Collins' usual standards, 120 cms by 90 cms. This is appropriate for the subject matter, however, in which extreme violence and innocent truth mingling with self-giving love meet. The historic occasion of Christ standing before Pilate has been remembered by the artist but universalised into Christ, the spirit of truth, innocence and love, which is the image of the Fool, confronted by his inverse image – earth-bound, angry and destructive. Grey, white and violet alternate and mix to give a glowering and

1. *Cecil Collins*, p. 83

gloomy tone to the picture, scored by a scalpel on its surface, but there is some relief at the top where the white, which cannot penetrate the aura of grey with which the Judge is surrounded, suffuses the stricken form of Christ. White is reflected also in the sea that can be seen lying in the background between the two large figures that face one another. The sea is a symbol of Spirit.

Everything about the Judge is angular, harsh and restlessly strong. Mechanism is very much in evidence in his whole form. He sits on a machine-like seat that can be propelled by wheels as if he and it together were a tank. His clawed right hand holds a script that could be the barrel of a gun. His spectacles look like goggles, and his mouth is distorted to reveal bared teeth. The helmet or headdress of the Judge is vaguely reminiscent of ancient, ignorant and malignant primitives. Critics have used the word 'Aztec', but this may be a slur on South American Indians. Five arrows that might have been long feathers point out of his headdress towards the ground to emphasise the source of his energy.

The form of Christ is straight with the marks of sustained violence evident everywhere. The head is crowned with thorns which nevertheless show the third eye and suggest the Trinity. The eyes are pits of sorrow and lines run downwards from the eyes and are reflected in the neck. The rest of the entire body is incised by lines marking the rib-cage, the arms, which are crossed as if tied at the wrists, and diagonally downwards along the robe he wears. His hands look like those of a skeleton but an uncowed power withstands the terrible assault and the eyes look up in a face more white than the rest of the body towards the symbolic white in the sky above.

This is one of the great sacred and religious paintings of the century. The verbal description of Christ that we discover in the New Testament and creeds are melted into a narrative that is iconic. The power of the Spirit is tested but not broken by the power of evil. So it was in Israel two thousand years ago, so is it now in other parts of the world.

Apart from paintings where recognisable Christian iconography is employed much of Collins' work, exactly because it draws on traditional and universal symbols, is not only sympathetic to the Church, it expresses in some measure what the Church expresses. Thus Kathleen Raine considers a 1968 masterpiece of his and declares, '*The Angel of Flowing Light* depicts a single monumental being whose eyes express at once knowledge, sorrow and judgement, but in a mode utterly remote from the human. Such a figure, too powerful for any secular art-gallery, should be in a shrine dedicated to St Michael and All Angels, were there any such church, whose dedication to the Angels was more than nominal.'[1] That this painting once in private hands has been bought by the Tate Gallery does credit to the secular and discredit to the ecclesiastical. It emphasises also the waste in opportunity afforded by the work of Collins and how Collins must have judged the visionless quality of the contemporary Church.

Something must be said about Collins' prowess as a teacher of art. It was part of his sacred ministry. Having asked Mr Robin Baring, a practising artist who was an early student and long-standing friend of Collins to supply me with personal recollections, I find that his script stands on its own and I reproduce it here. Those interested can place the words in context by reference to Anderson's biography.

'I studied with Cecil Collins at the Central School of Art from 1955–1959. I think he had been teaching there since 1952 so I must have been a relatively early student in his classes. My experience of his teaching is therefore limited to this period. However his teaching life unfolded without a break for a further thirty-four years until shortly before his death in 1989.

'He believed that art had a spiritual function and that it was the artist's purpose to reveal these spiritual qualities. He knew that the actual experience of creativity as well as the craft should be transmitted from generation to generation so that the roots of the present generation of artists were nourished in a living tradition not only by masters of the distant past but also of the immediate past. I mentioned the spirit of creativity above and I think Collins put this at the centre of

---

1. *Cecil Collins Painter Paradise*, p. 23

his teaching philosophy. He realised that no amount of expertise in craft, in knowledge or in art theory, however well taught, could by itself, produce a living work. Much of his teaching method was therefore directed to encouraging the actual experience of creativity. He wished to create an atmosphere in which he could awaken his students and infect them with the creative spirit. He believed that a good teacher could do this. There is no doubt that he had a charismatic presence in the classroom. The technical exercises, more evident in his Life Drawing Class perhaps than in his Composition Class, were largely the means by which he achieved his aim. But he was extremely articulate and spent a great deal of time in conversation with his students both individually and as a group; constantly pointing them towards different cultures and different historical periods and ideas, encouraging the possibility of broader and deeper philosophical perspectives than those offered by modernism. He believed the mind must be prepared and that this would help in bringing about the right attitude to the work.

'The atmosphere of his classes was extremely serious but punctuated at regular intervals by his enormous sense of fun and his apparently endless fund of funny stories, some of them extremely ribald. The majority of his stories, including the ribald ones, contained profound philosophical truths usually relevant to the work we were doing. It surprised me at first that a man who looked so ascetic and in many ways withdrawn from the world could have such a good sense of humour. His classes were impressive. He spoke with great authority and his teaching techniques were constantly surprising. At the same time he had an unusual level of empathy with his students. He seemed to have an intuitive insight into their characters and their problems. He was sometimes critical but with a gentle humour. Through his warmth towards his students and his sensitivity to their needs he seemed to draw the best out of them.

'Collins' teaching was derived primarily from music which in many ways was the great love of his life. He often said that he would rather be a composer than a painter and he loved to improvise at the piano. His knowledge and love of musical form was the foundation of his teaching method.

'At the time I was working with him he had two classes, one for Composition and one for Life Drawing. His Composition Class usually started with a short talk in which he introduced the subject matter of the day's class and discussed the problems and the techniques we would be using. Sometimes he would read a piece of poetry and ask us to produce a composition based on it. Sometimes we would arrive to find him setting up a still life which would be our subject. At other times the exercise might be much more abstract. While we worked he would usually move around the class talking to individual students and helping them with their work, sometimes he just looked at what you were doing and then passed on. In general his teaching in these classes was about the construction of form and the placing of forms in the painting. There was particular emphasis on the use of rhythm and movement, intervals, repetitions, inversion, the bridge passages and finally texture and colour. (The technology of his teaching continuously revealed its origins in music). He taught colour by a method which I think he had evolved himself called Triadic Harmony. In this system a palette of eighteen colours is used like a keyboard. The colours are divided into major and minor keys. They are then grouped in threes (triads) rather like musical chords and can be used, either in their pure state, superimposed or overlapping etc. The number of different triads which can be obtained from the original eighteen colours is enormous and of course each one carries its own specific emotion. The number of different harmonies that can be produced is almost endless, and by mixing triads at random surprising colour harmonies can be created which would have been almost impossible to arrive at in any other way.

'Occasionally, and unexpectedly, having set the lesson he would retire to his table in the corner and apparently take little further interest. He would produce a crumpled note book from his overcoat pocket which he proceeded to fill with indecipherable notes. At the end of the session he put all his papers back into the pocket of his overcoat. This he wore summer and winter no matter what the temperature. In winter he put a mackintosh over the top of the overcoat as well.

'It was, perhaps, in his Life Drawing class that his genius for inventing teaching techniques showed itself to the full. The room was large and rather warm to accommodate the model. The walls at each end of the room were hung with a double tier of framed reproductions of master drawings by Michelangelo, Leonardo, Raphael, Durer, Rembrandt, Goya, Ingres, van Gogh, Rodin, Picasso and Matisse. Either the morning or the afternoon session would consist of technical studies which Collins directed himself. The other half of the day students would draw without interruption while Collins directed the model and the length of the poses. He would often begin with a short walk in which he discussed the properties of the instruments we were going to use – pencil, pen – often quill, chalk, charcoal or brush and Indian ink. A warm up period usually followed and he would make us shut our eyes and feel the instrument with the fingers of both hands, test its weight and then make marks on the paper trying to search out and feel its character. This was done with eyes shut as well as open. Sometimes the warm up period would include listening to music, not only European classical music, but contemporary music as well and often music from the Far East and India. It was played on discs and an ancient portable gramophone which Collins wound vigorously. He would tell us to transcribe the music as it was played into visual terms with pencil, pen or brush and ink on paper to broaden our understanding of visual rhythm and phrasing.

'After this the real session would begin. The length of pose would vary from the long analytical pose of perhaps 1 to 2 hours to sessions of short poses of just a few minutes down to 10 seconds and less. Studies from the model would be done exploring the character of phrasing and phrase length, the pressure of the instrument, studies using the left hand only or using both hands at once with a different instrument in each hand or with the eyes closed after a short period of observing the model with them open. In these short poses anatomical exactness was not what he was looking for, but the living quality of line and mark. These techniques were designed to bring the student's sensitivity and nervous system into a state of high alertness. The shortness of the poses precluded any conscious attempts to do 'good drawings'. You just had to throw caution to the winds and allow the faculties to function and follow the flow as it happened. It was at this moment that you sometimes found that the drawing suddenly seemed to be appearing without effort and without your conscious intent, relegating you almost to the role of an observer. The ego's attempt to keep control, to try and repeat old patterns however successful they may have been, were defeated and the creative instinct was freed to function in the moment and without constraint. This was exactly what Collins was looking for and he was very quick to recognise which students were working from their true centre, producing work of real authenticity, and those who were still working from the ego with conscious effort. The debt to Zen philosophy in his teaching method, at least at this stage in his career, was very marked.

'It was not by any means every student who could accept or even wished to respond to this sort of teaching and I can remember a number of students who reacted strongly against the exercises and their originator. These students simply left the class, a very few walking out with a good deal of ill humour in the middle of them. Nor did Collins believe that his teaching was for everyone for he openly accepted that it could only be for those who found that they could benefit from it.

'Sometimes if he felt the session was not going well and everyone was trying to do good drawings he would stop the class, make us move one seat to the left and complete our neighbour's drawing. For those who were in love with their own talent and their work it was quite traumatic to find someone else ruining their drawing, but for others it often led to a breakthrough and you learnt that you were not necessarily there to produce good work, although that was very often the end product, but to get in touch with, and learn to have confidence in, the creative centre of your being.

'At the time I was there the teaching staff at the Central School of Art were drawn from a wide spectrum of artistic backgrounds; from the academic to the latest forms of modernism. They all taught according to their talents and their interests.

'I don't remember any rumours of rivalry or opposition to Collins' teaching. He had the total backing of the Principal, William Johnstone, who had invited him to join the staff in 1952 and of Morris Kestelman, who was Head of Fine Art, with whom Collins had a long and friendly relationship. It was only later that staff relations became strained at the school, when the teaching of art sank increasingly into the mire of politicisation under the leadership of the Inner London Education Authority.'[1]

PETER EUGUNE BALL (b. 1943)

Peter Ball was born in Coventry in 1943. His father worked in a car factory and among the options facing Ball in early manhood, married already at the age of nineteen and short of money, was to follow his father's lead. But his comprehensive school had brought out an innate love of poetry and visual art and the romance of the centuries that we call history. He had attended Coventry College of Art from 1957 until 1962 and immediately afterwards he joined a local historian in surveying Anglo-Saxon, Norman and Gothic architecture and its decoration. About this time he recalls first carving driftwood: 'It was in the Scilly Isles, it was 1960. I found a a little bit of driftwood there, and I worked on it; I carved something on it. I began to find there was something between the driftwood and me. I found it was a good way to work. It was simple, direct.'[2] He speaks very warmly of Southwell Minster and the deep impression made upon his sensibility by that ancient cathedral and its wonderful Chapter House. Romanesque inspiration and form find in him, though he never imitates, a natural ally. Celtic art and, of the moderns Picasso and Jean Debuffet also claim his admiration.

1. Author's archive
2. *Studia Mystica*, vol VIII, no. 4

One of Ball's first exhibitions was in 1963 with a group of artists at the Herbert Art Gallery in Coventry. A year later he took part in a number of exhibitions at Midlands Contemporaries, Nottingham. By this time he had introduced himself to the redoubtable Marjorie Parr and she, with an immediate appreciation of what he had achieved and could achieve offered him regular space in her London Gallery. She told me how he would drive up on his motorbike and produce a small sculpture from a bag and ask her opinion. It is testimony to her intuitive eye that she responded enthusiastically but the anecdote tells us something about the artist. He is rightly proud of his roots and suspicious of the bureaucracy, class interest and the vulgarisation of art resulting from the inter-action of commerce, fashion and those critics whose concerns may be various. For a time he lectured in Sculpture at Lanchester Polytechnic at Coventry. His first church commission was for a Crucifix at Westminster Cathedral, London and in 1975 he became free to devote all his energies to sculpting. Through the Gibert-Parr Gallery he gained exhibition access to a stand at the International Art Fair in Basel and gallery exhibitions followed in London, Holland and Switzerland. His work was taken to Basel, Dusseldorf, New York and Chicago through the auspices of international art fairs, and in 1981 he was able to spend six months travelling widely in Europe looking at art and gathering cultural impressions.

Peter Ball's first marriage ended in divorce but in 1982 he married Elaine Kazimierczuk. He had two children by the first marriage and two by the second. Since 1990 he and Elaine had lived in Newark, Nottinghamshire and he has shown work in Remetschwiel, Germany, the Basel Art Fair, 'sHertogenbosch in the Netherlands, the Alwin Gallery, London and in Houston, Texas. For a month or more each year he and his family live in their house on the Loire Valley in mid-France. Church commissions have formed an important element in Ball's artistic production. Some of the more important of these include a memorial at Preston-on-Stour Church, 1981, a crucifix and figurative candleholders at Birmingham Cathedral, 1983, a small crucifix for Portsmouth

Cathedral and a large Christus Rex for Southwell Minster, 1987; a Christus and Pietà for Winchester Cathedral, 1990; a Madonna and Child for Southwark Cathedral, 1990; a Light of the World, a Saint and a Christ Condemned (on loan) for Southwell Minster in recent years, a crib, Holy Family, Shepherds and three kings for Winchester Cathedral, 1991.

In 1995 Peter Ball was one of over 500 applicants for a major commission at St Nicholas Cathedral, Newcastle, and one of 129 artists who made detailed submissions. Eventually the competitors were reduced to Stephen Cox and himself and eventually Stephen Cox's submission was chosen. Perhaps the choice was correct but it would be interesting to know if it could have been different without the guiding hand of Northern Arts. Ball's Welcoming Christ was not only figurative but inspired by medieval iconography. Cox's fine circular form, suggestive of a eucharistic wafer and symbolic of deity is less confessional and more in harmony with modern abstractionism.

At the moment of writing Peter Ball is creating an altar, free-standing, figurative candleholders and reredos for the Silkstede Chapel, Winchester Cathedral, in process of being renovated. For some years he had served on the FACs of Southwell and Lichfield dioceses.

A second important source for artistic expression lies in myth, story and imagination. Ariel, Messenger, Harpy and Victim (numerous), the Ship of Fools (numerous), Pliny the Younger and Muse, Mermaid, Demeter, Daphne, Acrobat, Trojan Horse, Mummy Bundle (numerous), Satyr, Stiltman – or men (numerous), Fool, Death and the Maiden and Agamemnon give some idea of the subjects covered. Images such as Pilgrim (numerous) bring together the old Christian tradition and the less defined world of myth and story.

In conversation Peter Ball will sometimes affect an attitude which seems at variance with the deeply felt and sacred attainment of much of his art. He will lean on a Madonna and Child and talk about 'the damn thing' in reference to a crucifix. Asked point blank by a Roman Catholic priest involved in a joint commission for a liturgical piece, who had clearly been surprised by the breadth of Peter Ball's vocabulary, whether or not he was a Christian, the artist replied, 'No!' Analysis of the social attitudes of each of us is clearly difficult and often improper, but this idiosyncrasy seems worth pondering. Involved, I believe, is an exuberant personality, that needs relief from time to time, from the high but narrow concentration of much of his professional work and waking preoccupations. But more is included. We live in a secular and somewhat commercial culture and Ball's work is alien to governing drives in that culture. A down-to-earth manliness bridges the gap, not least in relation to the mores of his youthful culture. Centrally, however, I believe that Ball's nonchalent extraversion is an effective means of preserving his creative freedom, of guarding the sensitive and sacred fire in his breast. Dogma, institution, the representative significance of the priest suggest constriction, convention and conformity. His attitude is the same to what he calls the art world. So far as may be possible he keeps away from it. Fashion, the lure of money, the dominance of the gallery, critic or purblind art lover all constitute so many traps to the realisation of deeply felt imagination in sculpture. The reader will recall the outburst of Picasso recorded earlier on the subversive character of art (p. 114).

Examination of the sculpture of Peter Ball indicates the material used is often wood or metal used already, from a building, in a junk shop, out of the sea. He says, 'I have, since I started to make sculpture, used found objects, predominantly driftwood. My most recent work still retains this method of working although the subject matter has broadened. All my work is figurative, drawing from ancient and more recent mythologies.

'A friend once suggested that in my sculpture the seawashed driftwood, worn down to the hard grain, had left nothing but the essentials and that something like this seems to have happened to the images I make from it; they are reduced to the essentials too, as though the years had stripped away the rest.

'I am interested in the fact that these pieces of driftwood have been through many lives, first as a tree, then as part of a ship or whatever, objects which were originally designed with one function in mind end up serving quite a different purpose.'[1]

Thus the artist witnesses to the fact that the very material he uses is part of his final artistic statement. Its primary worn shape may even suggest the final statement. The softer portions of wood may have been washed away by the sea, leaving the hard grain, and defects in the wood occasioned by bruisings or insects may enable a perception of a particular kind of body. One of his extraordinary crucifixions began with a poor piece of a beech branch, battered by circumstance. Contemplating it, however, Peter Ball saw how this forked piece of wood could be the trunk and arms of Christ, how the defects could suggest the dereliction of Christ's condition and the arms describe the exultation. The end result was a theologically profound statement of the crucified and risen Christ in one. The artist recognises that such a statement, whilst historically just, is also perennially true and can be true of ourselves. He said, 'The deepest truth I have discovered is that if one accepts loss, if one gives up clinging to what is irretrievably gone, then the nothing which is left is not barren but enormously fruitful. Everything that one has lost comes flooding back again out of darkness, and one's relation to it is new-free and unclinging. But the richness of the nothing contains far more, it is the all-possible, it is the spring of freedom. In that sense the faith of loss is closer to joy than to despair.'[2]

Worn wood is also wood reduced to its essential and the concern of Peter Ball's art is with essence; Ariel, the Fool, and Christ are archetypal figures, their historical location does not exhaust their significance. Again, it is scarcely accidental that Peter Ball uses common things to produce the uncommon, as if there is analogy between earth and heaven. He declares, 'I think art has a purely spiritual significance. I don't use that word in any religious way. I just use it of a kind of experience that's on a different plane from ordinary

---

1. Quoted from Ingo Gilbert, *The Sculptures of Peter Eugune Ball*, p. 11, Speedwell Books, 1993
2. B. Leaman and E. Robinson, *The Image of Life*, p. 51, Revised ed. 1980, CEM/RMEP

experience. Yet it can reflect ordinary experience too – as religion does. In fact the more you think about it, the more similar they are, art and religion, I mean.'[1]

A reflection on Ball's understanding of the limitation and difficulty of words comes from his remarks on some of his gathered sculptures. 'They're very quiet, these figures, aren't they? They don't shout at you. It's as though they were mutes. This silence, I think it's something very important, more important than any statement. They may not speak, but you're aware of something coming from them all the same. Jesus was like that, presumably. Without his even speaking there was that presence. People were awed by it.'[2] Hence his unreadiness to make a verbal statement of belief. Priests may not understand, Christ does.

Let us consider two examples of Peter Ball's religious and sacred art, his Christus and Pietà, both located in Winchester Cathedral. The Christus is about 152 cm (5 feet) high and the arms stretch to a little less than the height. It is made of oak wood extracted from a house in process of demolition, a cross-beam that suggested the trunk and outstretched arms of a man. The long thin robed trunk is a device that goes back to ancient Syrian representations, the dislocated left foot and elongated embracing arms are his own invention. Pierced hands and feet are traditional. The gold, green and brown colouring is typically that of Peter Ball, involving the careful application of brass, copper, gold leaf and paint. The deity of Christ is suggested by the gold applied to the head, and the resurrection by the gold hands, feet and body markings. These circular whirls are not only effective; they take their origin both in the cloud formations of van Gogh, which have a sacred import as part of his generally sacred perception, and from the markings on ancient neolithic monuments. Christ is thus conceived not simply as an ecclesiastical figure but cosmically, as adumbrated by the gospel of St John.

The sculpture hangs from the north central wall of the

1. Op. cit. p. 50
2. Op. cit. p. 52

north transept about 6 metres (20 feet) from the ground. It had been made for Dorchester Abbey but some in authority at the Abbey were unhappy with such an image and it came to Winchester on temporary exhibition. The impact was immediate and a generous donor bought it for the Dean and Chapter. As hinted earlier I believe that something of mystery relates to sacred art and I suspect God destined it for Winchester where, like a wounded butterfly it came to rest and no one could disturb it. The Cathedral's Advisory Commission tried to do so, believing that the image intruded on a pure Romanesque area of the cathedral. Since the Commission could only advise the Dean and Chapter was able to listen to the advice but follow its own understanding. Its siting seems wholly appropriate.

No verbal description can do justice to authentic sacred visual art. The wisdom of Ball's general method of working with basic gestures to achieve an understated effect works here extremely well. Dispensing with a cross on which Christ would normally hang, because the significance of the cross is included in the form of the body, is part of this admirable economy and the compassion and aloofness, the suffering and deity, the crucifixion and resurrection make an unforgettable visual statement abreast of the best of contemporary verbal theology. Some of Peter Ball's own words about the Preston-on-Stour crucifixion make suitable comment on this piece. 'I've always been interested in a Christ that's compassionate yet aloof, like the Romanesque Christ, almost hieratic; not quite involved with humanity yet representing them. To me this is not an agonized Christ but very calm; compassionate but almost resigned.' And again, 'This detachment, it's a way of coping, recognizing human pain and suffering but not being destroyed by it. After all, you can't offer anybody anything if you're destroyed by what you see, can you? There's lost of suffering in the world, there are lots of poor people, there are millions of people starving all over the world. Yet before you can come to terms with all this, you have to be aloof, detached from it. Then perhaps you may be able to give something back.

'There's something of this in the Christ there. In a way he's saying, "I'm finished with you"; and yet he's also saying, "I'm giving you hope, this hasn't destroyed me". That what it's all about.'[1]

The Pietà came also to Winchester Cathedral in 1990. The local Roman Catholic community, who worship in the Cathedral from time to time, wished to make a contribution to our life and a sculpture for the Lady Chapel was suggested. The Catholic parish priest and myself worked closely on the project. The subject clearly included the Blessed Virgin Mary as she relates to Christ and a competition among invited artists was conducted. Peter Ball was selected and he produced a number of maquettes for us to consider. The catholic priest and I hoped that the Pietà would be chosen as this subject is rarely displayed in Anglican churches and yet it touches a note of profound archetypal and human truth. The authorising bodies agreed to the piece and the FAC were happy with the choice. We were confirmed in our desire for a Pietà by two events which occurred soon after authorisation for the commission was granted. Peter Ball's younger brother died and the grief of the occasion was poured into creative expression. After the Pietà was unveiled the Clapham rail disaster took place. Commuters from Bournemouth and other places well within the pastoral concern of the cathedral were thrown into experiences akin to that of Mary holding her dead Son. Television and newspapers showed pictures of people sitting with hurt or dead persons against them or on their laps. For months after the installation of the sculpture many people were to be found standing or kneeling in its vicinity. Though the form of basic images may change the essence simply recurs.

It took the artist five weeks to make the sculpture, though he had an assistant for part of the time. In distinction to the other artists whom I conducted to the site he seemed to look into the Chapel for a brief moment and took no measurements. No general conclusion can be drawn from such a fact but it testifies to the extraordinary visual intelligence of Peter

1. Op. cit. pp. 58–9; see also *Studia Mystica*, vol. VIII, no. 4

Ball. In imagination he could see almost immediately the
sculpture in its context. When it was unveiled we found
that its colours matched those of the surrounding stained
glass, painted walls and altar and that its vertical linear
form blended well with the perpendicular architecture of
the Chapel.

Standing before the sculpture we recognize the artist's
indebtedness to medieval form and substance, not least in
the physically dominating shape of Mary. Such dominance
related to medieval exaltation of Mary, sometimes at the
expense of Christ, and the recognition that we come to the
severe Christ through a merciful Mary, refuge of sinners. This
last thought can be expressed to mean that Mary is the
symbol of the Church and through the Church we find
Christ. In figurative terms everything has been pushed back
to its essence. The face of Mary, the hands and bodies carry
echoes of the German expressionist sculptor, Ernest Barlach.
In consideration of the basic form Ball was conscious of the
beautiful Pietà created by the young Michaelangelo, now in
St Peter's, Rome. There the anatomically correct large body
of Christ is contained artistically across the lap of Mary only
by introducing flowing robes and spread knees for the
Virgin. To break the dominance of that supreme image Ball
did the opposite. Grief constricts, so the figures are taut and
unrelaxed. Such a basic form tends to give a vertically linear
direction which harmonises with the architectural style of the
Chapel. The left hand of Mary cradles the neck of Christ, the
right hand stretches palm downwards. The left hand is protective and supportive, the right hand both displays Christ
and seems to be trying to push back the pain that assaults
her. The left hand pointing up and the right hand pointing
down is also a motive common in eastern art, calling attention to the relationship between heaven and earth.

The grieving, mask-like face of Mary has caused dismay
among some used to the productions of ecclesiastical
furnishers or even, in this case, to the masterpiece of
Michaelangelo. But Peter Ball has made a valid expression.
Mary must have been an old woman when the crucifixion
took place. The last days in the life of her son, culminating

in torture and death must have broken her heart. All this is transmuted into art. The so-dead body of Christ is crowned with a regal, noble face, limply stretching backwards and painted gold. Mary is faithful and stoical. Christ is dead but God.

Peter Ball has strong words to say about the modern church. There is 'something missing in modern religion: modern religions, that is, that have modified their outlook. Even Catholicism, because it's modified its liturgy and doesn't use Latin any more, it's lost something. I think ritual plays a great part, it's part of the mystery'. The Church 'has developed into nothing more than a social institution. It's quite wrong; it's not catering for the spiritual side of man any more. It's catering for down-and-outs. All it's interested in is bloody cups of tea. That's fine, you know, but there are souls to be saved'. Asked how the Church should set about that he replied, 'by retaining the mystery. There's no mystery left these days. How can there be a God anymore? People have just intellectualised Him out of existence.'[1] And again, asked about education, Ball replied, 'That's one of the most inhibiting factors on people's creative abilities. Especially church education, you know, the established church. It doesn't give anybody any sort of spiritual awareness. I don't mean Jesus as a living entity; I'm not interested in that really. I'm interested in the symbolism of the thing. To be honest, it's inconsequential to me whether Jesus lived or not. What is important is the level which human endeavour can and does attain, which is through art. I believe the power of religion is in images that have been its inspiration.'[2] The crucial importance of the historical dimension in Christianity has been argued earlier, disagreement with Peter Ball on this point should not blind us to the main thrust of his remarks. His own vocabulary reflects the essential view also expressed earlier that the seeds of images dwell in man awaiting incarnation in the work of artists, and that these images need renewing with the passage of time.

1. *Studia Mysticia*, vol. VIII, no. 4, p. 31
2. Op. cit. pp. 19 & 22

MARGARET NEVE (b. 1929)

Margaret Neve was born in 1929. She was the first of three sisters and her father was a solicitor. Her parents had singular views, one of which was that children should be educated at home. Whatever benefits derived from this regimen Margaret Neve recalls that it necessitated an introversion and loneliness that was only combated with time. She loved her grandmother who used to accompany the girls to church. Neve has always been a Christian and as a child she reflects that 'our belief was our lifetime'. Her father loved painting and through him she was taught her first lessons in art and encouraged to pursue painting and to look at paintings. In the period of the Second World War and after it she went successively to the Wolverhampton School of Art, the Birmingham College of Art and the Royal Academy Schools. She was a highly successful student and loved her time at art colleges. She gained a scholarship to further her studies and practice for six months in Florence. During this time galleries were already showing an interest in her work and Roland, Browse and Delbanco took it regularly. Margaret Neve has always been a figurative artist. She sees the significance of abstract art but was only briefly drawn to imitate the popular American abstract work. Nor was she a social realist; a Romantic element suffused her canvases and boards and she numbers Joseph Hermann among those who influenced her when young.

She married in 1955 and was soon the mother of two children. She and her husband James fostered in addition a backward child. Margaret Neve speaks with great affection and respect of her husband and clearly he has been a wise and trusted support through all the problems to be faced by an artist who was also a wife and a mother. The moral significance of priority assumed importance. To begin with her husband had to find his way, her children be nurtured and launched into independent life. She gave herself with joy to these tasks but suffered the pain of interrupted concentration upon the absorbing vocation of painting. In addition to their London home the family had a cottage in the beautiful Welsh countryside at Dolgellau. The healing and inspiring balm of nature worked its miracles and she entered more deeply into the Wordsworthian perception of the sacramental vision of what her eyes beheld. Church going grew intermittent in the years following her marriage, but her love of church build-ings, especially when empty, as places in which to meditate remains. So does Bible reading and prayer. She speaks with particular enthusiasm about the psalms, their wonderful language, piety and strong imagery. 'Rainbows, torrents and thunder' she entones, and relates this preference to her admiration of the masculine element in humanity.

She began exhibiting with the Marjorie Parr Gallery in 1976 and continued when this became the Gilbert Parr Gallery. The ten-year frustration seemed to be over. The new beginning by illustrating children's books, then writing a children's story and illustrating it herself was transcended. The life of the artist had returned. But a new difficulty began to reveal itself. She had been trained to paint within a partic-ular cultural context. The art market had its inevitable demands. Contrary to all this was Neve's growing recogni-tion that she wanted really to be a painter of paradise through the context of landscape. In art history her greatest love was for the medieval Flemish school. She mentions van der Weyden, Memling and van Eyck. She relishes their preci-sion, bright colours, love of detail and religious reference. Their landscapes have gained her constant attention. In contrast to the somewhat disembodied achievement of the contemporary Italian painters she loves the earthy quality of Flemish art. Reflecting this quality is another love, the nine-teenth century German Romantic painter Caspar David Friedrich. At the Royal Academy she had painted an Annunciation but it had not succeeded. She had wanted to translate into paint scenes from Thompson's *The Hound of Heaven* but they never materialised. Now the deeper urge re-asserted itself and was not to be denied. In her crisis she wrote down her thoughts for her husband to read. Her crisis was resolved in his encouragement that she should paint as she pleased.

Marjorie Parr had remained a stalwart friend aware of the

quality of Neve's work. Just before Parr's retirement, despite difficulty with several galleries, she eventually found through Marjorie Parr the Montepelier Studio, later the Montepelier Sandelson Gallery, with whom she began showing in 1987 and with whom she has remained happily since. Thus the mature concern of Margaret Neve's work was only achieved in her mid-fifties.

Whatever misfortune may lie in this fact for the artist as a person it is unclear if her art has suffered. After all it is not the number of paintings that count but their quality, and a painter of paradise is called to a narrow and high accomplishment; nothing could be more important than their realisation, no art could more easily miss its way. Maturity may be an assistance.

The public seem to have made their decision in favour of the artist's accomplishment. Her first two exhibitions were a sell-out and her third, for which the prices were significantly raised, sold all but three. Margaret Neve has been delighted also to discover that many who buy paintings or even only see them write letters of deep gratitude and sometimes of a markedly personal nature. Sacred visual art touches people directly and profoundly, stirring in them joy and recognition of what words sometimes confuse. As the critic Alexander Fyjis-Walker observes, 'to the viewer a mystic religious purpose always seems to be uppermost, and some of her paintings can be mysteriously and profoundly moving.'[1]

The critics have not generally much remarked her work, but as we have noted earlier this in itself may not mean anything substantial. Critics often were themselves at art school, which may condition as well as liberate. They work for newspapers that have their demands, demands that are affected by the need to increase readership and be reflective of the mores of society. Margaret Neve has observed the distinction that must be made sometimes between when an artist must or should create and the social, non-artistic demands that may be made upon him or her. Exhibition art, she believes, can be likened all too often to a fair ground

1. *Modern Painters*, Autumn, 1994, p. 109

where entertainment is of primary importance. I happened to be gazing at the last exhibition of Neve's work when a well known young critic of a leading national newspaper came into the gallery. He was there only a few minutes, sauntering through the rooms and then was gone. The secrets of this artist's painting do not reveal themselves to the casual observer.

The generation of a painting begins for Margaret Neve out of doors and in the midst of nature. The basic architecture of a painting comes in an instant, arising from an intuitive perception of the deeper significance of the movement of a stream, the way two trees cross or hills unfold. A sketch is made quickly in a notebook and a drawing results from this. The translation of this into the finished work, however, is what she calls a 'slog'. It may take three months or more to complete a painting but, unlike Albert Herbert, she always knows when the final point has been reached. Most of her work is oil on board but occasionally she makes drawings. These are impressive, convincing works of art in themselves, which only Margaret Neve, among those who appreciate her work, is inclined to belittle.

Neve's mature technique in oil painting is pointillism. This technique was developed without reference to Seurat and Signon, though she knew of their method. She developed it first from seeing an illustration in *Private Eye* and used it when she was illustrating books, since the effect in repro-duction on the printed page was so striking. A miriad dots, like tiny lumps on close inspection, comprise the coloured board. Seen from a distance this method of work gives a defined and exact edge to every object in a painting. A lumi-nosity is created and a curious stillness. The flowing rhythm of van Gogh, the open, undefined shapes of Albert Herbert are not in view. As one who spent the first third of his life in the Lake District I can report that Neve's creation is rare and authentic. Involved in such a judgement is the acceptance, even if only imaginatively, of the sacramental reality of nature. Constable's record of landscape is of mundane reality. Neve's record is sacramental of a higher life. At its most successful it is anagogic. Hence the absence of breeze, the unearthly stillness that those who have scaled Helvellyn to see the sunrise in summer and look with eyes of the kind possessed by Wordsworth will recognise: the still point in a turning world. I quoted Traherne to the artist, but she did not know the reference. 'The corn was orient and immortal wheat, which never should be reaped, nor was ever sown. I thought it had stood from everlasting to everlasting.'[1]

Another reason for her kind of pointillism is that it readily takes on the virtue of jewels. I looked with Neve at one of her paintings recently and foolishly exclaimed, 'why is that speck glinting?' I had not appreciated that in certain conditions of light the glaze at a particular angle on one or some of the points would reflect the light. Jewels do the same and the effect is brilliant and lively. The jewel-like effect has its place by reference to the old Flemish artists, possibly also because Neve is a woman, but in addition, I suggest, because jewels have been selected by mystics as types of the Kingdom of God. We recall the Early English poem 'Pearl'. We recall the later writings of William Law where he picks out the jewel as an object more than mundane, shining with a light more than itself. Traherene continues in the passage just quoted, 'Boys and girls tumbling in the street, and playing, were moving jewels.'[2]

Such work needs prolonged attention, not only that we may read it but so that it can take us beyond ourselves and it. For this reason the young critic saw but did not see the paintings at her exhibition through which he sauntered. Sister Wendy Beckett understands the requirement of these icons; 'Neve uses a demanding technique for her work, multitudinous dots, each a tiny glimmer of brightness, each able to be seen as separate or as blended, according to our position. Like the tiny budded trees, the Seurat-like dots have a cumulative significance. This radiant world of interior order, with its promise of a path to a heavenly angelic world, is achieved through labour. Neve prays her work into existence, into holy meaning by hour after hour of fine-tuned

1. *Centuries*, III, 3
2. *Centuries*, III, 3

flicking with the most delicate of brushes. Hour after hour, day after day, she summons into visibility her mystic sheep and the world they offer to share with us. If the work takes long to paint, it equally takes long to view. Only after contemplative attention may we notice that the trees are not uniform. The nearest tress, the trees on our side, as it were, are closed. But the distant trees, the trees on the angelic side, are opening.'[1]

Images recur in the mature art of Margaret Neve: the angel, the hill, the sheep, the tree, the lake, the boat, the sun, the light, the journey, the clouds, the rainbow, the flower. Sheep are strikingly recurrent from the Welsh countryside, obvious tokens of innocence and prominent in the Bible. Adam and Eve and the Blessed Virgin Mary also find their appearance. A riveting country scene with sheep, hills, mountains, trees, sky and clouds is named *Altarpiece* (1994). In the vocabulary adopted in this book I would say that the artist is open to the archetypes within herself and embodied in nature, that nature and her contemplative mood stimulate this deeper life and, in conjunction with her artistic perception the architecture of a painting is suddenly born. Showing her a reproduction of *The Cliffs and Downs* (1994) where beautifully stylised sheep, hills, trees, clouds, sea and sun make up a single composition I said provocatively, 'No actual landscape looks like this', to which she rightly replied. 'But that is what I saw.' This same landscape painter is not in thrall to Constable.

In *Mary and the Archangel* (1994) Neve achieved her youthful ambition of painting an Annunciation. The scene is a typical Neve landscape. In the foreground there is a gentle lake with reeds at the border where land begins. Two hills meet towards the centre of the horizontal line of the frame, rising towards its outer edge. In the background is a luxuriant forest of trees. A line of trees not yet in blossom mark a pathway along the frontal plane of the picture just behind the reeds. Their line is echoed in a bank of clouds that

1. Sister Wendy Beckett, *Art and the Sacred*, p. 56. Sister Wendy is considering Neve's painting, *Trees of Gold*, 1989

almost line the top of the painting. The blue and pink of the sky suggest that dawn is coming. The archangel Gabriel is a major focus of the composition. He floats above the ground just left of centre. His feathered wings are like a great opening flower, seen from below. Their shape describe a circle with the shoulders, head and arms of the archangel moving forward outside the circle. The right hand is gently raised in blessing for Mary, a diminuative figure, sitting in a boat floating on the lake. She is dressed in white and looks up towards Gabriel. Gabriel is large, strong and masculine. His whole form is coloured red and a speckled stream of red dots flow from his mouth to Mary. The meeting is erotic but not physical, she conceives in love but her love is not sensual, her whole self is given over to the divine who wills this miracle. The mystery of the impregnation of Mary is neither sullied nor analysed. Enough is represented to honour both God and human ways.

Margaret Neve is a notably shy person. I asked her once about her debt to the early medieval painters. She said quietly, with tears in her eyes, that they gave her 'permission to paint'. She believes that a great deal separates their achievement from hers. We may decline to be sure about this last point.

ALBERT HERBERT (b.1925)

Patrick Reyntiens described Albert Herbert as 'the most significant religious painter to emerge in England during the 1980s'.[1] In a letter to the author the distinguished American abstract expressionist painter, Robert Natkin, declared, 'I believe Albert Herbert to be one of the very few four or five great artists alive today. Within this very short list he stands out as number one as a painter of the highest redemptive art. I believe that this group of paintings called "The Stations of the Cross" are of universal appeal, beyond catholicism or any other Christian institution. Although the subject matter deals extensively with the pain and suffering of Jesus, Albert

1. *The Tablet*, 11 November 89

Herbert's stations all resonate with the thrilling joy of the resurrection.'[1] According to Sister Wendy Beckett 'no one who sees his work (Herbert's) can doubt that we have here that rarest of phenomena, the great religious artist'.[2]

The son of a window cleaner in the east end of London, Herbert's father lost his work during the blitz. As a boy he remembers thinking that a glade must be a holy place and that one should bow to a tree. Young Herbert joined the army and was present at the Normandy landing as an infantry man. At the end of the war he was given a grant in 1947 to go to the Wimbledon School of Art; from there he won a scholarship to attend the Royal College of Art. Friends and fellow students included John Bratby, Peter Coker, Derrick Greaves, Edward Middleditch and Jack Smith. He exhibited with them in a form of social realism known as Kitchen Sink. This had nothing to do with socialism and everything to do with a fairly factual recording of one's environment which, for most of these men of modest background, included humble work-a-day scenes. In 1951 he married Jacqueline Henly, a RCA sculpture student, by whom he had three daughters. A Royal College of Art travelling Scholarship took him to Rome, where he was introduced to Renato Guttuso and other Italian realist painters. He felt at this time the charm of Italian Catholicism and, a little later, visiting a Catholic monastery in England felt curiously at home. He became an art college lecturer, successively at Dudley, Birmingham and finally at St Martin's, London, 1964–88, being made eventually Principal Lecturer.

In 1958 Herbert became a Roman Catholic. There was no dramatic conversion. He described the process to me as similar to the discovery by a homosexual of the true nature of his sexual orientation. He had received no religious education when young and he had no personal interest in religion until his thirties. Looking back, however, he can find in his thinking and painting hints of what was to come. Catholicism was and remains for him the way of truth rather

1. Author's archive, 6 December 91
2. *Arts Review*, p. 772, November, 1989

than the truth itself, an institution with tradition and fine ritual. At first his new religious affiliation did not affect his painting. The impact of American abstract art was being felt in Britain at this time and there was an assumption that to be contemporary one had to be an abstract painter. Herbert felt he had to swim with the stream although he is inherently a figurative artist. After a year he stopped painting and only resumed it after a ten year period in which he did much etching. St Martin's was the most avant guarde art college in England and Herbert, with typical modesty, thinks that his senior appointment was due partly to the knowledge that as a Roman Catholic and erstwhile figurative artist he had deep cultural roots and could help restore and retain some kind of balance amid the ungoverned experimentalism of the time; an interesting reflection considering the previous argument of this book. Herbert thinks also that his whole generation of artists 'had some wound inflicted on it' by the artistic irrationality that was then inescapable.[1]

In 1976 Herbert visited Thailand and South Korea at the expense of the British Council, teaching and looking at art schools. He was impressed with Buddhism and eastern spiritual thought, but his Catholicism, which had been somewhat marginalised was renewed, without losing empathy with other religious expression. He has said to me that he might have been a Quaker but that ritual seems to him very important, or he might have become Anglo-Catholic had circumstance been different. In other words he recognises the importance of the institutional element in religion and the fact that institutions point beyond themselves into the sublime, ineffable mystery of God. Herbert reads theology with interest and critical acumen and his understanding of the Incarnation would seem to be similar to that expressed in this book.

As the 1970s turned into the 1980s he began to ask himself why biblical subjects might not be painted. Herbert's own words tell the story: 'Over the past ten years my subjects have been taken from the Bible. I have done this as a

---

1. Robert Macdonald, article Albert Herbert, *Modern Painters*, pp. 81–2

discipline, as a way of escaping from a private world of self expression. The Bible stories are treated as symbols, metaphors, revealing the "marvellous", an intention which I first discovered in that surrealist magazine long ago. I began to think of traditional images in the Bible, which allied me to all those other European artists who had been doing this sort of thing for the past 2000 years.

'I have no interest at all in the historical factuality of these Bible stories, but I have read many theological interpretations of them and the paintings can be read in different ways. Like icons, they have symbolic meanings. Theology helps me to understand my personal experiences, but in a way I want to make paintings that are more public and easier to understand although there is a side of them that is very private. When I met Sister Wendy Beckett she said that "these are images of something below the level of consciousness ...".

'... Paintings do not have meanings that can be put into words. It is true that I usually start with some idea that can be put into words but when I begin to paint I become entirely involved in the difficult process of making a painting. The struggle to harmonise shapes, colours and textures is worked out on the canvas. This can go on for months. The original idea becomes lost in the paint and re-emerges as something quite different, and usually much more interesting.'[1]

During the period when the change in his painting was about to emerge Herbert found that surrealistic imagery began to appear. Hidden theological data would present itself, such as the division of an etching into three parts or the word DOG which is, of course, God in reverse. As the change progressed mythological ciphers became increasingly Christian imagery. After his abstract period he found that he had to learn again how to master the figure. This he did by drawing or painting as a child. The figures became more sophisticated but only in the sense that a growing child's imagery changes. It is typical of Herbert to prize for

---

1. Albert Herbert, *Recent Paintings, Introduction*, pp. 3–4, 1994

examination crayon drawings by his grandchildren. Notable
in his paintings is the remaining abstract quality of the blocks
of paint. They can be read as patterns by those who choose
to do so.

Whilst a painting with Herbert usually begins as a literary
idea, at some stage, as suggested in his own testimony just
quoted, he touches a deeper level of the imagination and
together with the problem of painting the pressures of the
archtypes make themselves felt. It is no surprise that he has
been fascinated by the story of Jonah and the whale. The
dramatic biblical legend reflects many age-old elements of
myth as it mirrors recurrent features in our own lives.
Humans are burdened with a mission from which they try to
escape but cannot. We are thrown into the sea, engulfed by
a huge fish and vomited onto dry land. The difficult mission
is discharged. From the legend of Gilgamesh this kind of
story repeats itself in cultural and personal history. A
painting of Albert Herbert depicts the Crucifixion; the Cross
is green, the right hand of Christ stretches sympathetically
downwards, the Tree of Life grows luxuriantly behind the
Cross, a man kneels to pray beside it, and a woman's face
looks out of the painting at the viewer. In conversation
Herbert said to me that the right arm of Christ simply
adopted a downward position but that he did not know why
it did. I suspect that his own sympathetic nature and his
perception that Christ was the Incarnation of love were
features governing its composition. The rest is a universal
statement of historical fact and myth. The well known device
of artists to have one face looking out of the picture is suit-
ably here a woman, being an image of the soul. She involves
us in this life-giving drama.

Similarly, Herbert's *Eve in the Garden, Jonah in the Whale,
Noah in the Ark and The House of God* is shaped 60 x 20 cm
(23½ x 8 inches) so that we may read it from the bottom up.
We begin with the age of innocence, proceed to the drama
in the sea within the belly of the whale, from thence to
Noah's Ark and then to the Church. Historically the Ark
comes before Jonah, but for the emphasis on God's saving
grace juxtaposing of Ark and Church is triumphantly correct.

The pattern of colours with their browns at bottom and top, blue in the middle and golds and reds interspersed must be seen to be relished aright and as part of the picture's statement.

Mention has been made of Herbert's interest in theology and the literary origin of many of his paintings. This intellectual element in the total production of a painting is worth consideration. Recently he was telephoned and asked to exhibit in a mixed exhibition at a London church where Angels was the general subject. Herbert replied that he did not think he believed in angels. Positing them seemed to suggest a dualistic universe. He was asked to put his thoughts on paper and send a painting in any case. After some thought he wrote as follows:

'I have read that in the first century pagan world it was a common belief that we might encounter the gods in human form (the apostle Paul and Barnabas were mistaken for the gods Zeus and Hermes by the people of Lystra). So no one would have found it incredible at that time that an angel appeared to Mary. But a lot has happened since then and most of us now find it really difficult to integrate into our imaginative world. Personally, I can only see the traditional image of a robed, winged, genderless angel as a once powerful, but now obsolete symbol. But a friend tells me that she is not sure about God, but knows that she has a guardian angel. I respect her experience but prefer to interpret this "angel" as part of her own psyche, wiser, above ordinary consciousness and perhaps a bridge between time and eternity. This is not the orthodox view of angels but it is not a very long way from the medieval idea of "angelic consciousness". Angels, having no sense organs, were supposed to have a different form of consciousness. Some theologians thought that we too possessed this "angelic consciousness" and by meditation could develop it.

'I decided to work out my confused thoughts about this by trying to paint an Annunciation. The only way I could honestly represent the angel was as a woman looking exactly like Mary, as if in a mirror, so that they are not two but one (like everything else).

'It is all I can do but I am not happy with it. IT IS TOO influenced by Jungian theory which is already beginning to look obsolete. The idea that religious phenomena comes from our own psyche is really very introverted, almost solopsistic – the old theology of angels, although quite fantastic, was assuring us that we are not spiritually alone in the universe.'[1] From such cogitation, Herbert produced a beautiful painting along the lines described in his writing and in the space of a few hours. Like Collins I would take a more traditional view of this subject but the archetypes find expression through, as well as despite, our conscious minds.

In 1987 an enterprising Anglican vicar approached Herbert with the prospect of a commission to produce 14 Stations of the Cross. Herbert was thrilled to think that some of his work might find place in a church and dutifully created a number of detailed sketches 35.5 x 28 cm (14 x 11 inches). Jesus falls under the Cross, Jesus is Laid in the Sepulchre, and the rest. They were created in oil on board and were strikingly original, expressionistic and devout. One that shows the mocking of Jesus depicts leering faces emerging from the darkness, with clutching hands near him, whilst Jesus has a dismayed face, but the tearing off of his white garment makes his whole image like a flower blossoming in a harsh environment. The Parochial Church Council rejected the offering as too "disturbing". Patrick Reyntiens commented shrewdly, 'They are beautiful and moving and one wonders if there was not too much experience and truth in them to be other than disturbing to the congregation using them for devotion. This unhappy example of incomprehension and alienation on the part of prospective clients shows up all too clearly the hazards and the near-impossibility of effecting commissions of true quality within the consciousness of the Church, however much the goodwill towards such activities is claimed to exist.'[2]

1. Author's archive, 1995
2. *The Tablet*, II, November, 89

END PIECE

Brief consideration of the work of these four modern artists indicates the vitality and contemporaneity of sacred and religious artists. Together with their accomplishment we note their wrestlings and difficulties. We note also that they speak to those who can see, of God, in immediate and convincing manner, expressing what words cannot say. The Church has made some effort to embrace the modern artist but there remains historical luggage to drop and a broad vision to discover before the mission of the visual artist within the Church is recovered.

SELECT BIBLIOGRAPHY

W. Anderson, *Cecil Collins*, Barry and Jenkins, 1988.

W. Beckett, *Art and the Sacred*, Rider, 1992.

J. S. Begbie, *Voicing Creation's Praise*, T. and T. Clark, 1991.

T. Burckhardt, *Sacred Art in East and West*, Perennial Books, 1967.

A. Chastel, *Art in the Italian Renaissance*, 1988.

G. D'Costa, *Theology and Religious Pluralism*, Blackwell, 1986.

J. Dillenberger, *Style and Content in Christian Art*, SCM, 1986.

John Dillenberger, *A Theology of Artistic Sensibility*, SCM, 1987.

E. Duffy, *The Stripping of the Altars*, Yale University Press, 1992.

J. Epstein, *An Autobiography*, Art Treasures Book Club, 1955.

J. Gimpel, *The Cathedral Builders*, Pimlico, 1993.

V. Haggard, *My Life with Chagall*, Robert Hale, 1987.

P. Hetherington (trans.) *Painter's Manual*, Sagittarius Press, 1974.

W. Hussey, *Patron of Art*, Weidefield and Nicholson, 1985.

H. W. Janson, *History of Art*, 4th ed., 1991.

R. C. D. Jasper, *George Bell Bishop of Chichester*, Oxford University Press, 1967.

B. Keeble (ed.), *Cecil Collins, The Vision of the Fool and Other Writings*, Golgonooza Press, 1994.

A. Liberman, *The Artist in his Studio*, Thames and Hudson, 1988.

L. Ouspensky and V. Lossky, *The Meaning of Icons*, New York, 1983.

P. Pace, *The Architecture of George Pace*, Batsford, 1990.

E. Panovsky, *Meaning in the Visual Arts*, Penguin, 1970.

E. Panovsky, *Renaissance and Renascences in Western Art*, Icon, 1972.

G. Pattison, *Art, Modernity and Faith*, Macmillan, 1991.

K. Raine, *Cecil Collins*, Golgonooza Press, 1979.

K. Raine, *Willian Blake*, Thames and Hudson, 1970.

K. Raine, *David Jones*, Golgonooza Press, 1974/5.

P. Reyntiens, *The Beauty of Stained Glass*, Herbert Press, 1990.

E. Robinson, *Language of Mystery*, SCM, 1987.

E. Robinson, *Icons of the Present*, SCM, 1993.

L. Rodley, *Byzantine Art and Architecture*, Cambridge University Press, 1994.

T. Roszak, *Where the Wasteland Ends*, Faber, 1972.

J. Sahi, *Stepping Stones*, Asian Trading Corporation, 1986.

P. A. Sorokin, *The Crisis of Our Age*, 1941, One World, Oxford, 1992.

R. Temple, *Icons and the Mystical Origins of Christianity*, Element Books, 1990.
Theophilus, *On Divers Arts*, Dover Publications, 1979.
E. J. Tinsley, *The Imitation of God in Christ*, SCM, 1960.
O. Von Simson, *The Gothic Cathedral*, Pantheon, 2nd ed., 1962.
K. Ward, *Religion and Revelation*, Oxford, 1994.

INDEX